The "It" Factor

KEEPING IT REAL...

Bobette Stubblefield, M.S. ed

ISBN 978-1-965951-24-8 (Paperback)
ISBN 978-1-965951-21-7 (Ebook)

Inquiries and Book Orders should be addressed to:

Seraphim Global Media LLC 155 Willow brook Blvd Ste 110
Wayne, NJ 07470
848 800 6538
info@seraphimgml.com

The "It" Factor
KEEPING IT REAL...

Bobette Stubblefield, M.S. ed

Table of Contents

The "It" Factor
K EEPIN G IT R E A L…

This book is dedicated to all those who have struggled with loving yourself, loving others, and (sometimes) loving God. I want you to know …
you matter.

Writing this book was a laborious journey. I am especially thankful to my family. Throughout my life, you were an integral part of my journey. You challenged me to be the strong woman I am today. Mom, you taught me to hold my head up …

no matter what I was going through.

Michael and Matthew, I am proud to call you my sons.

To my spiritual sons and daughters, thank you for all your help with dad and the dog as I labored over these pages.

To "Mongo", my partner, my friend, my husband …
I love you MORE.

Foreword...
THE "IT" FACTOR ... KEEPING IT REAL

Important life lessons are often fully realized long after they occur. Much of what I learned about life and business came from two young boys who wanted to make some money. On this particular Florida spring day, I happened to look out the kitchen window and saw my two young sons busily gathering things and placing them into a shoebox. Curious, I hollered out and asked, "Boys, what are you doing?"

With a slight southern drawl, they answered in chorus, "We're collectin' frogs. We're gonna sell 'em and make lots of money!"

The teacher in me determined it was a good time to have a lesson in economics, so I called the boys over to the stoop and sat down with them. After examining their fine collection of tree frogs, I asked them, "What are you going to do with these frogs if nobody buys them?"

Their faces crinkled as they pondered over the absurd idea that maybe not everyone would buy their frogs. "Well ... we could keep 'em, Mama."

I thought for a moment and finally answered, "Yep. You could, but they're going to have to live in the backyard."

They weren't very happy with that idea as boys (who are likened to slugs, snails and puppy-dog tails) like to treasure their critters *in* the house.

In an effort to redirect their disappointment and encourage the entrepreneurship spirit in them, I held out the box of frogs and said, "Boys, I love the idea of you wanting to work and make money. There is, however, a little thing called 'Supply & Demand'. What you need to do is find something people want. When they want something, that creates a demand for it, and they will buy it."

After much deliberation, my eight- and nine-year-old boys decided that everybody wanted homemade chocolate-chip cookies. Not only was this an opportune time for a math lesson (recipes are great for teaching fractions), but I was more than happy to let those poor little frogs free!

In their new business, the boys hired me to help them make the cookies. We all scrubbed up, donned aprons, and set about the task of doubling the Tollhouse recipe. After a few hours, we completed the measuring, mixing, blending, and baking process and the aroma emanating from the house/factory smelled like money!

They carefully packed four mid-size cookies to each Ziploc bag and loaded them into their little red wagon. We then sat at the dining room table and worked through the difficult task of determining the cost of making the cookies versus the anticipated profit margin. The boys finally decided that $0.50 a bag was a fair price for their product (in the late 80's, this was a reasonable asking price).

We then took a few moments to change into outfits that people would want to see if they had a salesman at their door. The boys decided that it would be better if I did not come to the doors with them, but my new job would be to pull the wagon and wait in the road. We spoke a blessing over the business and headed out!

The lady at the first house they approached happened to give them $1 for the bag of cookies. Unbeknown to me (in the road out of hearing range), the price of the bag of cookies just went up to $1. House after house, the people paid $1 for each bag of cookies (I just thought they were being generous).

Then, after giving their sales pitch at one house, the lady happened to give them $2 for the bag of cookies. Once again, unbeknown to me, the price of the bag of cookies just went up to $2.

We worked our way up one street and down another. However, when the boys ran up and knocked at this one particular house, there was no answer. So, they knocked again. No answer. I hollered, "Come on, boys, evidently no one is home."

My youngest son, Matthew, turned and hollered, "Mama, I can hear somebody in there!" And they beat on the door again.

Inching closer, I loudly whispered, "Boys! Come on ... let's go the next house."

Obviously agitated, Matthew turned to me again and loudly stated, "Mama ... there's somebody in there. I can hear 'em!" And, they beat on the door again.

By this time, I was within hearing range. After one more series of knocks, the door opened and there stood a not-so-happy man wrapped in a towel. My sons immediately sprang into action. They proudly displayed and pointed to their bags of homemade chocolate-chip cookies and proceeded with their sales pitch.

"Sir, my brother and I decided that all people want home-made chocolate-chip cookies. We made these fresh cookies today and they can be yours for only $2 a bag." (To myself, I thought, *$2 a bag*???) "How many bags would you like?"

The disgruntled man looked down at them and said, "I don't have any money." Then he dismissed them by shutting the door.

My son, however, shoved his foot into the crack and with his free hand pushed the door back open. Boldly, he said, "Sir. My dad often throws money down on the floorboard in the car. I bet if we go look in your car, we can find $2."

I was mortified. This man, however, was impressed. Before I knew it, they had this towel-wrapped man at his car while the boys searched for change on the floorboard. In the end, they found $2, and the man received his bag of homemade chocolate-chip cookies.

I wish I could say that I continued to encourage these two young entrepreneurs after that. Instead, this young mama failed miserably in earning the "Mom-of-the-year" award. I shut the business down – embarrassed over the brazenness of my sons. Years passed before I realized the valuable lessons I learned from two of the finest young men in my life. They taught me things like:

▶ If the market is willing to pay $2 for a bag of cookies, then you sell them for $2.

▶ A "no" answer isn't rejection.

▶ Find a way. Where there is a will, there is a way.

▶ Persistence.

Some of us give up way too early. We encounter an obstacle and lose heart. Such was the twelve-year on again/off again journey of writing this book. The initial dream was planted in me at sixteen years old. I knew then that God wanted me to teach people that their lives matter. "It" matters to Him that we learn how to be real with ourselves, real with others, and real with Him.

Forty years later, I am finally pouring out my last words upon these pages. Some of the lessons took a lifetime to learn, maybe because I needed to trust the value of brokenness. Along the way, though, I have found out that broken people "smell" good. I rarely trust anyone who has not been broken.

Other lessons were gleaned from those who traveled the mountains of difficulty before me. To you, I owe my life. The many times when I wanted to quit, your words scribbled on the pages of my old Bibles and on the scrap pieces of notepaper tucked here and there have served to sustain me. In this book, I have tried my best to give credit to those of you who had an influence on who I am today. If I have missed accounting your work to your name, please accept my sincerest apologies. There were many old, scribbled notes throughout my Bibles that I simply failed to write down who said it. Even though your every word is chronicled in Heaven, I earnestly desire to give you credit as well. Please contact me (www.bobettestubblefield.com) and I will make every effort to correct my error.

If this book helped you find that place where you can live wide, open, and free with yourself, with others, and with God - I also long to hear about your journey to "real-ness". The way we live really does matter to God. Without saying a word, people should be able to look at the way we interact with others and from that, know the whole gospel story.

Your life ... "it" speaks volumes to the ones reading it.

The "It" Factor ...
Keeping it Real
CHAPTER ONE

———————◦———————

"Beloved, let us love one another
For love is from God;

And everyone who loves

Is born of God and knows God.

I John 4:7 (NASB)

Jesus had a unique way in which He taught His disciples deep spiritual truths by using practical, real-life situations and stories such as; The Prodigal Son, The Marriage Feast, and The Ten Virgins. He didn't just tell them word stories for entertainment purposes, but He developed them into recognizable word pictures associated with common-day traditions so that people would remember them. The spiritual applications were meant for the practicalities of this life as well as teaching them something bigger, something beyond themselves.

I call this the "It Factor". "It" is bigger than "I". "It" is grander, higher, and more inclusive than my little world. I am limited, but "it" is all encompassing. Sometimes we don't exactly know what "it" is. For example, "it" often kept me in line as a young person -because I didn't want to get "it" when I got home. I didn't know what "it" was, but I definitely didn't want "it"! Later, as a parent, I threatened my children with "it" if they didn't behave.

"It" is the all-inclusive *something*. "It" draws you to that little peep- hole in the fence around your life and invites you to look *beyond*. "It" is your way out of the forest when you are only looking at trees. "It" is the BIG PICTURE.

When life closes in on me and I can't see past my own pain, I pray for the ability to see "it" – the things happening around me through God's eyes. "Help me to get 'it' Lord". There's something bigger going on in this situation that is crushing me. Help me to see 'it'." Nine times out of ten, He leads me over to the spiritual peephole and gives me a glimpse of what He sees. Of course, there are times that He does not show me – because either I don't really need to know, or I am simply being too obstinate in my hurt. Over time, though, I have learned that there are certain matters that are near and dear to His heart, and He doesn't mind showing me what is going on in the Big Picture or the Grand Scheme.

One of the dearest matters of His heart is that of relationship and marriage. Paul, in Ephesians 5:32-33 states, "This mystery is great, but I am speaking with reference to Christ and the church. Nevertheless, let each individual among you *love*...[1]"

When "it" comes to relationships, there is indeed a bigger / grander picture. Our lives tell a bigger story to the ones who are watching and listening. *My* life was eternally impacted by the actions of one man, at a particular moment in time, on an unusually warm winter day in south- west Georgia...

My husband, Jesse, and I had recently moved from Seattle and were thrilled to have purchased an old Plantation home on the outskirts of Cairo,

---

[1] New American Standard – The Hebrew-Greek Key Word Study Bible. ©1984 and 1990 by AMG International, Inc.

"The Hospitality City", of Georgia. It had been built back in the 1800's and the old-timers say that it was one of the first in the area. Throughout his- tory, though, owners of the property sold off section by section until it finally bordered the city on a large lot. For us, it was a sweet taste of the South. The property still had the old servant's quarters, 18th-century architecture and a BIG old pecan tree! That first season it put out the best pecans I had ever tasted! I was thrilled!

The next two seasons, however, the tree produced nothing – except a perpetual MESS! (I can always tell the Southern people in an audience about this time because their heads begin nodding in agreement.) When early spring comes and the tree begins its dress for summer, catkins (3-4 inch cylindrically shaped, light-as-the-air, male pistillate 'flowers') cover the tree in wait for the March winds to take them on a journey of polli- nation to the awaiting female pistillate star-shaped 'buds'. For weeks, anyone near a pecan tree sweeps, rakes, or blows millions of these catkins off covered vehicles, driveways, and yards. When the male pollination season is over with, the tree will then expunge the star-shaped virgin female pistillates. There is a brief reprieve until late summer when the tree begins to lose its leaves and/or fruit. The nut is enclosed in a thick, green husk that turns black and splits into four parts at maturity. For each nut, there are four unsightly husk pieces that litter the ground. Once again, the owner is out cleaning up debris – leaves and husks – while gathering that sea- son's fruit.

Needless to say, I was overjoyed when autumn arrived, and the tree stood bare that third season. That is, until the birds showed up that year. A large flock of blackbirds made that one tree, the one that hung out over our driveway and parking area, their winter home. It wouldn't have been so bad, but they were eating red berries somewhere, then perching above the parking area and dropping red concrete-like bird dung all over my car!

It's not like I was driving any kind of vanity statement. My car was a 13-year-old 1988 Oldsmobile 88' that my biological Father had given me a couple years prior to help us get back on our feet after an uninsured drunk driver hit my husband (another story for another time). When it was given to us, it really needed a paint job, so Jesse scraped together as much money as he could and paid for a nice maroon professional job. In my eyes, it was beautiful. I appreciated the car and took good care of it and Jesse knew that, so he kept promising me that he would wash it.

At the time, I was working full-time, and my husband was running a business and working as a pastor some 30 miles away in Tallahassee. If it wasn't the business, it was the church needing him six or seven days a week. Our schedules were slap full and sometimes the simple task of washing a car was a major event in our lives.

But there happened to be one Saturday, an unusually warm winter day, when I found myself caught up with all the household chores and a yearning to spend some time outside. As I looked out the window, my eyes caught view of that horribly globbed-up car. It was then that I decided to help my husband, who at the time was in Tallahassee tending to church business. So I grabbed the hose, filled a bucket with soapy water, and diligently began wetting the car down. When I thought it to be sufficiently wet, I proceeded to scrub at those stubborn globs, that to me, resembled concrete. They wouldn't budge. So, I gave the car another thorough soaking. Still, they would not soften enough to wash off.

Then I had a great idea. I knew what would remove those stubborn spots! I ran into the house and next to the kitchen sink, retrieved my little green 'scrubby'. (I know, I know. In all the conferences I have spoken at, this is the time when all the men groan!) And, sure enough, within seconds I had removed the first of the hundreds of red concrete globs!

With that, I held the hose close and gently scrubbed off each one of those stubborn globs. I started with the hood, then worked my way over the top and finally onto the trunk. Just as I finished the last one, I looked up as Jesse drove into the driveway. In jubilation, I stood proudly at the back of the car, threw my hands out and said, "Honey, look what I did!"

The look that came over his face was NOT a good one. There was not a hint of an "atta-girl" in it. Hesitantly, I turned around toward the car and took in what he saw. By that time, the vehicle had started to dry and as I scoped from front to back, I saw what he did – literally HUNDREDS of little white circles where I had 'scrubbied' the paint right off!

There was a moment, however brief, that we were speechless, and it seemed the world stood still. My mind raced with a thousand thoughts – a thousand words. I could hear the words of all the men in my life up to that point ... "You will never amount to anything! You hear me? You are nothing! You are stupid! *You* are the problem! You are worthless!..." And I braced myself. I thought, "Here it comes... here it comes..." I dropped my head and waited.

What my husband did still reduces me to tears. He walked my direction and stopped in front of me. Gently, he scooped my head up so he could look me in the eyes. Then, he said the most loving words I had ever heard ... "Maybe we can buff them out."

A dam broke loose somewhere deep inside of me. He held me close as I wept deeply. Neither one of us knew it at the time, but God took this simple act of a good deed gone wrong and turned it into one of life's great spiritual lessons.

You see, for the first time in my life (and I was almost 40 at the time) I had a glimpse of "Abba Father" – not the condemning judge, just waiting for me to screw up – but Abba who truly loved me! That incident paved the way for a healthy relationship between me and my Father; one that is not performance based or derived out of fear. Through my husband's actions, I now knew Grace.

That day, as I stood at a little peephole in the fence around my life, I got a glimpse of "it" – the bigger picture. God used a man, a human vessel, to represent Himself and extend healthy relationship to me. The whole scenario was a means of healing my broken heart, mending relationship, and opening my eyes to a larger story. You see, up until that event, I had always assumed relationships and marriage to be a list of to-do's and not-to-do's and *if* we did everything right (i.e. *if* he loved me like Christ loves the church and *if* I respected him…) then God would be pleased and maybe even bless our home. Relationship was exclusive and private and watched over by a very distant and judgmental God.

However, after the good-deed-gone-wrong incident, I had a glimpse of something bigger, more inclusive. I set out on a seven-year search for answers and a twelve-year endeavor of writing this book. I hope you will join me at the peephole as we discover the "It Factor" in relationships.

At the Beginning...
CHAPTER TWO

"Then the Lord God formed man [the human] of dust from the ground,
and breathed into his nostrils the breath of life;

And man [the human] became a living being.

and the Lord God planted a garden toward the east, in Eden;
and there He placed the man [the human]

who He had formed."

Genesis 2:7-8 (NASB)

Come with me to that fence called 'life' and let's take a stroll over near the beginning. I'm sure God wouldn't mind us getting a peek at His original design. Find yourself a comfortable peephole – there appears to be a few way over there, as we are not the only ones trying to get a glimpse of what God is up to – countless numbers of angelic hosts are curious as well.

With the dawn of this new day, all of heaven is anxious to see what Elohim, The Creator, was up to next! They whisper among themselves about His previous handiwork – the establishment of the heavens, complete with sun, moon and constellations; as well as the formation of the earth regulated by the complex simplicity of nature. To them, the Creator's interest in this earthly domain has been quite fascinating. His attention to every detail, from the smallest microbe to the fine-tuned rotation around the sun, has kept them all wondering what could possibly be next.

As we peek at the Creator's back, bent over His new project in the earthly wind-blown wilderness, we can overhear whispered conversation along the fence line…

"What do you suppose He is up to now?"

"I don't know. But whatever it is, He's keeping it hidden for some kind of grand presentation, I guess."

"He seems to be a bit … weary. After all, He has just finished making a physical world, complete with heavens and an earth full of life…"

"…and this life has the ability to reproduce itself!"

"Does He look tired to you?"

"Yeah, He does. But, even more than that, He looks … well … *labored*."

"He does seem to be laboring much harder over *this* project."

"And look at His hands – they are covered with dirt forming this one."

"Not only His hands, but *He* is covered with the substance this one is made of!"

"Look! He is hand-fashioning a form…"

"Shhh…."

They watched intensely, eyes glued to the portholes, as Father was taking great care in the fashioning of this creature. After a brief time, the whispering resumed…

"It looks to be about His size."

"He sure is taking great care in forming this one."

"Hush! He's determining… *purpose*."

"Listen to Him moan…"

"That is the deep calling unto deep – with sounds that cannot be uttered."

"Look! He is pulling out from his ... inward parts!"

"You're right! He seems to be extracting elements of Himself and fashioning them *into* that creature!"

"Everyone, be quiet! Whatever He is creating is causing Him great labor. He looks as if He's put His whole heart into…"

"…wait! What is He doing now?"

There's a long pause as they watch Almighty God prone Himself over the creation. His Spirit hovered over the figure for the longest time.

"He's got that look again."

"Yeah – it's as though He is *longing* for something…"

"No, I think it's for ... *someone*."

"I've seen that look on Him before."

"You know, I've no doubt that He loves us – but I think there is someone He desires more intimately- one more like ... *Him*."

They looked away from their peepholes for a brief moment and glanced at each other.

"That could only mean…"

"That what He is pulling out of Himself is not only His attributes and likeness, but ... like Him, this one will have free will!"

"This creature – whatever it is – will have the freedom to choose!"

"And to dream, create, express…

"…and ... have free access to the Creator!"

"What *is* this creature?"

"*Who* is this creature?"

When they peered back through the fence, they witnessed the Creator lovingly take hold of both sides of the creature's head, then from the depths of His Spirit blew life into the nostrils of the still form. The angels held their breath – waiting.

Suddenly, the creature gasped and jerked awake! The heavenly host jumped back from their portals, exchanged surprised looks, then scurried back up to their vantage points.

Still positioned in front of this 'being', Father knelt, took its appendage in His and pulled the being up to a sitting position. They gazed at one another. Father must have had a big smile – as the creature strangely contorted its face in an effort to mimic the Creator.[2]

Father threw His head back and from His belly came laughter that sounded like the melody of all beings and all time merged into one. With that, He helped His creation to its feet; then turned to face the multitude of heavenly hosts eagerly peeping through the portals. With a loud voice, He declared, "May I present to you – the last of my creations – Adam!"

At first there was a loud roar of laughter for "adam" literally means "human". To the understanding of the angels, this sounded to them like, "May I present to you …the human from the humus – or more literally, the earthling from the earth or dirt creature from the dirt!"

Adam and Father gazed lovingly at each other. The angels now comprehended the enormity and significance of this creation – Adam – and with a loud resound and applause, the hosts celebrated and sang their praise to the Almighty One, Creator of Heaven and Earth!

---

[2] Some theologians believe that Adam was born from the womb of God and raised from infancy to adulthood by God Himself. All this author knows is that everything is possible with God. It is possible that Ezekiel 16 alludes to the nurturing attribute of God raising a young child.

Then the Lord God formed man [the human] of dust from the ground, and breathed into his nostrils the breath of life;

And man [the human] became a living being.

and the Lord God planted a garden toward the east, in Eden; and there He placed the man [the human]

who He had formed."

Genesis 2:7-8 (NASB)

One of these details, easily overlooked is the fact that the first human, Adam, was created *in* the wilderness – outside of the Garden. Have you ever wondered how long he was in the wild mountainous outback? Genesis 2:8 says that God *planted* a garden, *then* placed Adam in the gar- den. How long did it grow before He introduced Adam to his new home? Was it already established and bearing good fruit? I have read accounts of some theologians who firmly state that each day of creation was a literal twenty-four-hour period and, therefore, within hours Adam was created and immediately placed in a ready-made garden. I am, however, more apt to think that it was *planted* as Genesis 2:8 clearly states, and each plant grew just as it does today. Then when it was presentable as a gift for Adam, God brought him there. To further substantiate this delay in the wilderness, Genesis 2:8 states that the Garden of Eden is *where* He ultimately placed the man. Genesis 2:9-14, however, describe *how* God planted the garden, purposely placing the tree of life and the tree of the knowledge of good and evil, and the rivers that flow out of the garden. (Genesis 1:11-12 also detail *how* the earth sprouted vegetation with seeds that bear their kind.) Finally, in Genesis 2:15, it states, "**Then** the Lord God took the man and put him into the garden of Eden..." Knowing God, the Father, I think He wanted to surprise Adam and present a beautiful new home to him – to be appreciated after the wilderness!

To support this determination, Genesis 2:15 continues, *"Then the Lord God took the man and put him into the Garden of Eden to **cultivate** it and **keep*** *it.* " The Hebrew word for cultivate is "abad" which basically means, "to be worked". There had to be something already there for him to "work" and "keep".

So how long was Adam in the wilderness? I think long enough to find out what it means to be a man! The man-boy (all of us have that little boy or little girl inside of us!) not only needed to discover who he was and his value in his Father's eyes, but he needed training on how to be a real man. I can almost hear the hoots and hollers as Adam shows off to God how fast he can run from this mound to that knoll – or how he was finally able, after a few hard falls, to scale that mountainside! I cannot picture Adam as soft or uncoordinated. Out in the rough terrain, he was able to hone his muscles, develop coordination, and learn to live in an environment that was bigger than himself. The outdoors will do that to you. If you haven't been fishing or camping in the past few years – try it again. There is just something about getting up on a chilly morning, hugging a warm cup of campfire coffee, and listening to the birds sing their songs. All of a sudden, life's problems don't seem so big, and creation calls our minds toward our Creator. Our mind-set changes from *me* – how pressured *I* am, how hurt *I* am, how people are treating *me* – to how big God is and how He has perfectly placed me as an integral part of His creation. Somehow, in those moments, the "knower" in us confirms that we belong in this big plan of His and we have purpose in our just *being* alive.

God gave Adam purpose after his wilderness training. Genesis 2:15 states, "*Then the Lord God took the man (the human) and put him into the garden of Eden to cultivate it and keep it.* "[3]

God so loved this human that He gave him PURPOSE! According to Webster's Dictionary, if something has no purpose, it is purposeless – or aimless. The intent of God's purpose for each one of us is to have us *work* toward *something* so that our life has meaning. The garden was not created to serve the human – it was to be worked by the human. He gave

---

[3] New American Standard – The Hebrew-Greek Key Word Study Bible. ©1984 and 1990 by AMG International, Inc.

the first human a JOB! The Word says that God is the giver of all good things; there- fore, work is good. This is a write-down. If need be, write it a thousand times – WORK IS GOOD!

God also gave us a good thing when He set boundaries in place. Years ago, I heard of a study where researchers observed the playing patterns of young children. When a fence surrounded the playground, the youngsters utilized the WHOLE area – even climbing on the fence. However, when the fence was removed, the children huddled in the center of the field because their safety was removed. We need boundaries in our life, they keep us secure.

Therefore, after determining purpose for the human – God set forth some boundaries. Genesis 2:16 says, *"And the Lord God commanded the man (the human), saying, 'From any tree of the garden you may eat freely; but from the tree of the knowledge of good and evil you shall not eat, for in the day that you eat from it you shall surely die.'"*[4]

Note that the Lord did not say, *"if* you eat from it…" But, rather, the Lord stated, "…for in the day *that you eat* from it…" From the foundations of the earth, God knew that man would indeed cross that boundary and eat from the tree. Did the human have a choice? Of course he did. But God the omniscient who sees the beginning as well as the end, knows us better than we know ourselves. He intimately knows our DNA makeup, thought patterns, circumstances, habits, curiosity levels, and everything else that determines our choices. To say that we are predestined in our destinations, only means that He who sees everything knows ahead of time what we're going to choose. That is why crossing this boundary did not take God by surprise and a redemption plan was already in the works for *"the day* [in which] *you eat from it…"* The proof of this is recorded in Revelation 13:8 which states, *"Everyone living on earth will worship it [the beast] except those*

---

[4]   New American Standard – The Hebrew-Greek Key Word Study Bible. ©1984 and 1990 by AMG International, Inc.

whose names are written in the Book of Life belonging to the Lamb slaughtered before the world was founded."[5]

An analysis of the Hebrew text of Genesis 1:1 confirms God's provision long before Jesus became fully human. It is translated, *"In the beginning God created the heavens and the earth."* Strategically placed in the very first line of the Hebrew scriptures is the Hebrew letters aleph and tav (Alpha and Omega – the expression meaning the whole Alphabet – of which Jesus referred to himself in Revelation 22:13.) This aleph and tav appear between the words "God created" and "the heavens". Therefore, it literally reads, *"In the beginning God created the aleph and the tav before He created the heavens and the earth."*[6]

Commentaries on this verse explain that putting aleph and tav together create a word that has no correctly translatable meaning. However, if one studies the ancient texts, the Hebrew alphabet was originally written using pictograms. The pictograph for the aleph is an ox – an animal often used in sacrifice. The pictograph for the tav is a cross – signifying a mark, sign, ownership, a joining together of two things and covenant! Therefore, God planned a sacrificial offering which is sealed with His Blood; long before man crossed that boundary and pronounced death upon himself!

So, keeping in mind the safety that boundaries provide, let's read this verse in its context:

Genesis 2:16-20 (NASB):

"And the Lord God commanded the man [the human], saying, 'From any tree of the garden you may eat freely; but from the tree of the knowledge of good and evil you shall not eat, for in the day that you eat from it you shall surely die.' Then the Lord God said, 'It is not good for the

---

[5] The Complete Jewish Bible. ©1998 by David H. Stern, Jewish New Testament Publications, Inc., Clarksville, MA.

[6] "Signs of Christmas – The Aleph and Tav" by Tiffany Ann Lewis 12-21-08 published by The Elijahlist.com

man [the human] to be alone; I will make him a helper suitable for him.' And out of the ground the Lord God formed every beast of the field and every bird of the sky and brought them to the man [the human] to see what he would call them; and whatever the man [the human] called a living creature, that was its name. And the man [the human] gave names to all the cattle, and to the birds of the sky, and to every beast of the field, but for Adam [the human] there was not found a helper suitable for him."

Note that after the Lord gave the human boundaries, He then spoke His next thought. His idea was that He would make another human for the man; for it was not good for him to be alone. But did He immediately make another human? No. Father God set about working His plan. Instead of presenting the man's counterpart, the Lord hand-picked animal-by-animal, *"every beast of the field and every bird of the sky and brought them to the man..."*

In chapter one, I briefly described the beautiful old Plantation home we had purchased in South Georgia. When we first bought this home, it was white with pink trim (as you can imagine, my husband said it was too "girly" and looked like a dollhouse) and everything was painted white inside – very plain. When the house was finally ours, we walked through and *said* our ideas; this wall needs taken out, this carpeting needs pulled up, this will be painted such & such a color... Now, none of this happened immediately. For it to be done right and for a full-effect afterwards, other things needed to happen first (money needed to be saved, materials purchased, colors coordinated, electrical upgrades, etc.).

The ideas were spoken; then we made them happen in an orderly manner. Within a matter of years, we were able to enjoy our remodeled home – mossy green with white trim, large rooms with archways and columns, restored wood floors, rich colors throughout. It took time, but we lovingly formed it with our hands.

The same is true about our Father. He spoke an idea, then set about taking care of the things that would enrich the experience of presenting another person to the man. First, the man needed to become *desperate* for another like him.

So, God immediately went to work hand-picking and presenting every beast of the field and every bird of the sky that He had formed from the ground. Now, I have heard all my life that God simply *spoke* and things happened – poof, and they magically appear! Although I firmly believe that He is fully capable of doing just that, I find more comfort in knowing that He is a hands-on God! David in Psalm 139 states that He *formed* my inward parts; He *weaved* me in my mother's womb, and I am fearfully, reverently, and wonderfully *made*! Genesis 2:7 says that He *formed* the human. The Hebrew meaning of the verb, to form, means that He squeezed us into shape to determine purpose.

When God went to work hand-picking each particular animal that He had formed from the dust of the ground, then proudly presenting it to the man, this took time. Furthermore, the man had to study the individual eating habits, characteristics, and mannerisms of that animal before he could name it. The man's job description was expanded! Not only was he responsible for cultivating and keeping the garden – his new title was "Namer-of-the-animals". This all took time! How much time? I don't know. But it was sufficient enough time that Adam (the man) became desperate for a mate of his own – for there was none suitable for him.

The Hebrew word actually used for this 'mate' or 'helper' (as it is commonly translated) is *ezer k'negdo*. *Ezer*, in the Bible, most often refers to when people called on God in their most desperate times. It in no way denotes inferiority or subordination. In fact, the true meaning of the word, *ezer k'negdo*, is one who is a 'life saver' or 'one who is equal to or like unto'.

Isn't it likely that if the new human was to be ruled by the first, God would have initially commanded it so?

Furthermore, why would God create this second human with anything less than the first? Was intelligence, creativity, or personality diminished with the next human? Were dreams or ambitions less import- ant – or nonexistent? Personally, I have NEVER in my life encountered a woman who has dreamed all her life of becoming a "helper". Quite the contrary! When us gals share our dreams, the world is limitless! Some want to be wives and mothers. Others dream of being doctors, lawyers, and business owners. Not one has even hinted that they want to be a "helper". However, ALL desire to be "Eight Cow Brides"! If you haven't read Patricia McGerr's story originally published in Woman's Day magazine in 1965 about the story of Johnny Lingo and his eight-cow bride, Sarita, it is well worth the research finding it! In a brief synopsis; Sarita is a very homely girl whose chances of gaining a husband are grim, much to her father's sorrow and the village gossips' delight. There is no man in the village willing to pay even one cow for poor Sarita. However, one day a handsome prince from a far-away land comes into town and sees Sarita's true worth. His gift of eight cows for this woman changes the entire village, including Sarita, who now walks with her head held high. McGerr's narrative is a captivating tale of our true worth in God's eyes. Women want to be eight-cow women!

In my professional career, I have managed businesses for over thirty years and when I hire a helper, I am filling a position that is entry level. It is the bottom-rung of the ladder. I can honestly say, I have never met a person who has dreamed all their life of becoming a *helper*. Yet, to hear the opinions of many men – we, as females, ought to be pleased that God "created" us to be "helpers"! As a woman, that devalues me. It makes me feel "less-than". There are some men that even infer that *they* are made in God's image, but woman came from *them*! However, the Word assures us that, "...God created man in His own image, in the image of God He created him; male *and* female He created *them*." (Genesis 1:27)

For Adam (the man) to call upon God for *ezer k'nego* – one who is equal to or like unto him, he was desperate. He wanted someone like *him*! He has spent countless days, weeks, maybe months or years studying animals and watching them court and mate their counterparts. Made in God's image, the human was created for relationship. God, in Himself, is in perfect relationship within Himself! The Father, the Son and the Holy Spirit are separate, yet one. There was something within the human that craved relationship with one that was separate, yet who is equal to or like unto him!

> "So the Lord God caused a deep sleep to fall upon the man
> [the human] and he slept; then He took one of his ribs, and
> closed up the flesh at that place. And the Lord God
> fashioned into a woman the rib which He had taken from
> the man [the human] and brought her to the man [the
> human]. And the man [the human] said, 'This is now bone
> of my bones, and flesh of my flesh; She [this one] shall be
> called Woman (*Ishshah*) because she was taken out of Man
> (*Ish*)." Genesis 2:21-23 (NASB):[7]

This is the first time in scripture that there is a gender specific. Man is now *Ish* and Woman is now *Ishshah*. God presented *Ishshah* to *Ish* after He had fashioned and prepared her. This is the first 'wedding'. According to Webster's Dictionary, a wedding is "to unite as if by the bond of marriage." The interesting thing is, when you 'marry' two pieces of metal together, it means you cannot tell where one ends, and one begins. The two literally become one. For this reason, the author of Genesis felt it important to include the following verse for scriptures' sake; "*For this cause a man shall leave his father and his mother and shall cleave to his wife and they shall become one flesh.*" (Genesis 2:24) How appropriate! In the beginning was a wedding; then, the ministry of Jesus started with a wedding; and in the end, "It" will all culminate in a marriage supper!

---

[7]   New American Standard – The Hebrew-Greek Key Word Study Bible. ©1984 and 1990 by AMG International, Inc.

Life is Good!
CHAPTER THREE

———————∽———————

"...and the Lord God fashioned into a woman the rib
which He had taken from the man (the human)

and brought her to the man (the human).

And the man (the human) said,

'This is now bone of my bones,
and flesh of my flesh;

She shall be called Woman (Ishshah)
because she was taken out of Man (Ish)."

Genesis 2:21-23 (NASB)

There is not one living soul who can convince me that when God presented the woman to Adam he *stoically* announced, "This is now bone of my bones, and flesh of my flesh; She shall be called Woman (*Ishshah*)…" But I have heard it preached in this non-passionate way for years. I can only recall two Pastors (my husband being one) who think these were NOT Adam's first words after he saw his counterpart. In fact, they insist Adam's first word was, "SHA-ZAMMM!!!!!"

To take it a step further, I even think Adam, in all his manliness, wanted this exclamation to come out sounding much like James Earl Jones or Clint Eastwood – a manly man's voice – but my imagination conjures up a pitch sounding much more like … Mickey Mouse. Having grown up in the wilds of Alaska, as well as raising boys, this qualifies me for a bit of "male" knowledge. What I do know is that the male species – whether it be horses or roosters – all attempt to "strut their stuff" for the gals! There is something programmed within the male that desires the pretty chick. Of all the guys I grew up with, not one of them ever dreamed about winning the ugly duckling. Nope. They all dreamed, planned, and desired to have *the* beautiful one on their arm. It is a non-verbal statement to the world, "Look at *me*! I am *something* because I obtained *her*!" Lord knows, my boys acted like fools around pretty girls! Our youngest was notorious for puffing up his muscles, spreading his chest as wide as he could and moseying around in his most 'manly' strut while girls were around! He wanted them to think he was *the* man!

The woman, *Ishshah*, was not just a nice addition to the garden set- ting – she was *the* woman! She was Adam's *ezer k'negdo* – the one equal to or like unto him in his most desperate time! In my mind, I picture God joyously surprising His friend with His new creation! Can you see the man? Over there … sitting relaxed in the soft grass after his 'surgery' just listening to the sounds of birds singing their songs in the trees and watching the squirrels chase each other, jumping from branch to branch. All he knew was that he had just woken up from the best sleep he ever had; however, he seemed to be a bit tender on one side, so he leaned over on his elbow. Beyond the ferns and hiding behind a tree, I see the woman, standing a little unsteady getting used to her limbs and practicing balance. She hears her Father's voice whisper in her ear, urging her to peek around the tree. "That is who I am going to introduce you to!" says the Father.

Her eyes widen and she peeks around for a second look. Father, enjoying this immensely, snickers as He says, "He has no idea! I can't wait to see the look on his face!" Then, He looks lovingly upon His beautiful creation – smoother, softer, and a bit smaller than Adam – and coaxes her, "Do you feel ready?"

Still a little unsteady, she takes a few paces back into the shrubbery, practices a turn then walks back to the hiding place. Taking a deep breath and holding back a giggle, she tells Him, "I don't think I can do this with a straight face – can I smile?"

Father can't help it this time – His new creature is so enjoyable – and He lets out a belly laugh. "Of course, my beloved, of course you may smile!"

Hearing Father's laughter, Adam calls, "Father?"

The time has come. So, Father excitedly whispers to the woman, "Wait here till I call for you." Then He stepped out from His hiding place and asked Adam, "My beloved, have you named any new animals today?"

"No, I haven't. The funniest thing happened … I fell asleep in the middle of the day! And, I must have fallen, as my side is quite sore right now!"

With a raise of His eyebrows and a big smile on His face, Father answers, "Oh, is it now? So, I take it you have NOT found someone like unto *you* this day?

"No." Adam lowered his head and picked at blades of grass, pulling them up one at a time by their slender shoots. "Father, I'm beginning to think there is none out there that is like unto me. Don't get me wrong … I love our time together and I love talking with you, but I can't help to think there is something *more* – am I making any sense?"

Still smiling, Father responds, "So, you are bored with these wonderful creatures I have made? Surely the monkeys entertain you? What about the platypus or the ill-mannered camel, as you call it? Do these not keep you amused?"

"Nearly every day. But, with exception to those pesky monkeys who like to throw things, all the creatures are pretty consumed with tending to their kind." Sullenly, Adam flicked a piece of grass and let out a sigh. "Something in me can't help but wonder if there is one like *me* who I can – you know …" and he waved his hand over the landscape, "share all this beauty and adventure with."

"So, you desire another human?"

Adam's eyes lit up as he considered the possibility of sharing life with another human being, but in order to clarify his request, he looked down at the grass again while he searched for the appropriate words.

"Well, actually… as you know, I …uh … have been studying the animals and their characteristics – that is, their … um … you know, their mating habits. And I was …" He earnestly searched for the right words to express the deep ache in his soul. *"Something – what was it – a profound and unfathomable thirst – a deep, deep longing for oneness – a mate to love, to touch and to be touched - a companion to share life with, to laugh with – to become vulnerable with…"*

As Adam struggled with his words and deep emotions, Father motioned to the woman, and she quietly stepped out from behind the tree – BIG smile and all! He then broke into Adam's thoughts and asked, "Adam, will this one do?"

Adam lost in his aloneness, absentmindedly asked, "What?"

"This one, Adam. Look!" Father couldn't wait any longer for the grand presentation.

Adam's eyes popped opened and involuntarily he back-crawled on all fours – both taken aback and trying to get up on his feet. The only word escaping his mouth was a very high pitched, "Sha'Zamm!!!"

A little embarrassed about how that sounded to his ears, he hastily composed himself and found a posture against the shade tree he had just scuttled up to that purposely highlighted his physique. He couldn't take his eyes off this lovely creature! Her smile captivated him. Her loveliness enveloped him. And her curves excited him!

Father was pleased! With that, He was gone … leaving the two of them to get acquainted. He would explain later how he birthed this woman from the man, forming her from one of his own ribs.

While the Spirit hovered over love's display, let's take our attention to the outskirts of Eden. Living there, in the not-so-nice section, is a shady character who took offense at his new neighbors taking up residence in such close proximity and obviously in close relationship with the Landlord.

Now, an old Chinese proverb goes, "Know thyself, know thy enemy. A thousand battles, a thousand victories." Had the first couple known the devious nature of their neighbor who happened to claim a little more than squatter's rights to their land, I doubt they would ever have trusted a thing he said. However, I can't point the finger very far. How many of us today are duped because we underestimate the enemy? How many of us have neglected the study of the one who seeks our destruction?

My curiosity about this shifty character was piqued one day as I sat in an Art Appreciation course at college. I happened across a painting by William Blake entitled, "Satan Watches Adam Caressing Eve." It so captured me that for the next two years I worked on a response to this image. Below is a poem I finished in January of 2001:

Heaven's Fallen Angel

Behind the depth of physics, where a mortal eye can't see,

Lurks Heaven's fallen angel, humanity's archenemy.

He bears the pain of Love's abyss, and glory days gone by,

He's ruler of this lesser world – still judged by Him on High.

This is not his ideal kingdom, and he resents this earthly place,

Roaming through the canyons, he recalls his celestial case.

Overall, he argued well, determined to defend his side.

First, he tried to show the Judge – it was simply misplaced pride.

Creation told Creator, "It was not a strategic coup!

Surely You are mistaken, it was wanting to be like You!"

Ultimately, he reasoned, "…It is *You* who bear the blame,

You placed me in a position where I received un-asked for fame.

May I remind your Highness, I *was* a faithful server …

It's really not my fault; I was simply caught up in fervor!"

As thunder clapped on distant shore, he remembered the gavel well.

The Judge's eyes shot fire, as He sentenced him to hell.

Sitting atop a near mountain, Lucifer considered his plight.

For a brief inexplicable moment, he thought the Judge to be right.

There was still a part of him, that longed for "Perfect Love",

The fullness of His Presence, he once enjoyed above.

Banished from the Heavens now, he surveyed the barren land;
Dismayed, he then decided, maybe he should plead again.

Starting for the Heavenly Throne, he neared the Garden Eden,
When he saw what God was up to, decided against the pleading.

Hidden under foliage green, Celestial blend with leaves,

He saw the full human-ness in the forms of Adam and of Eve.

While watching their caressing, he heard a voice say, "This is good!"
Then felt so very far away when from High the Heavens thundered.

Peering eyes formed narrow slits, as passions did ebb & flow;

With every tender caress, Pure Love enveloped mortal show.

Despite the Spirit's Presence, Lucifer began to seethe.

He could tell this mortal placement, put an end to his reprieve.

How dare the Supreme Being, ever banish him away –

But then now to have to watch Him abound in love's display!

Pain was more than he could stand, it pierced his heart like a knife.

He turned his head to hide the tear, as Adam caressed his wife.

Sorrow surrendered to hatred, as Satan devised a plan;

With raised fist to the Heavens, he vowed the falling of man.

Turning Love upon the Giver, he gleamed about the force.

More powerful than heated swords, he would turn it on the Source.

Looking back over his shoulder, he glared at *beloved* Adam.

"Go ahead and love her now – through her, you'll both be damned!"

Behind the depth of physics, where a mortal eye can't see,

Lurks Heaven's fallen angel, humanity's archenemy.

He bears the pain of Love's abyss, and glory days gone by,

He's ruler of this lesser world – still judged by Him on High.

To think that the enemy doesn't like you simply because you have a personality defect is utterly preposterous! In fact, it doesn't have much to do with you at all – save for a bit of jealousy. It has *everything* to do with his relationship with the Creator!

I love the line, "He bears the pain of Love's abyss..." That came to me in the middle of the night. I had a visual of a great divide – one in which Satan cannot step across. Although the Word states that he still has access to the Judge of the Universe – he has been thrown down![8] One can only imagine what it is like to dwell in the Presence of Love! We have yet to fully understand *who* Love is! The Word says, "Better is *one* day in Your courts ... than a *thousand* elsewhere!"[9]

To be banished from Love's presence is the ultimate punishment, pure torture! To even feel an inkling of what that may feel like, we can imagine the Prodigal Son. In his rebellion, he thought the grass was greener on the other side of the hill – only to find out how dark that place really was! He even envied his father's servants when he came to his senses. How many of us have angrily left homes or marriages, only to find out that it really wasn't so bad after all? In fact, we had it pretty good.

Like us, the Accuser may have held out for one last reprieve – one glimmer of hope that he could return to his former status. Knowing Love like he once knew Him, maybe there remained one last hope…if he only repents ...

Can you see all hope drain from his face as he comes up on Adam and Eve? All of a sudden, all the puzzle pieces fit together, and he knew there would be no pardon for him. It was a done deal. He was banished … forever.

As he peered through the foliage, I believe he caught a glimpse of the something bigger – the grand scheme. In the line, ***"But then now to have to watch, Him abound in love's display…"***

Satan knew that God was being glorified in the human's display of love. God was all over it – and it pleased Him. These humans obviously captured the Lord's heart.

---

8 Revelation 12:10 "And I heard a loud voice in heaven, saying, 'Now the salvation and the power and the kingdom of our God and the authority of his Christ have come, for the accuser of our brethren has been thrown down, who accuses them day and night before our God." Revised Standard Version

9 Psalm 84:10

Lucifer's heart turned black. Through narrow slits, he studied the couple and devised a plan to hurt the One who hurt him. Then, it dawned on him. There is nothing so powerful as the power of Love. Therefore, he would turn love back on the Source of Love; much like a deflected laser beam, he would inflict damage upon the Giver. Yes, that was it! How to hurt the heart of a Father? Turn His children against Him or destroy them. Either way, humanity – the pinnacle of God's affection – became involved in a war they could not see. For, in the spiritual realm, "it" was bigger than them.

Life is … an Adventure!
CHAPTER FOUR

―――――⌇―――――

"And by the seventh day God completed His work

which He had done;

And He rested on the seventh day

from all His work which He had done."

Genesis 2:2 (NASB)

The declaration of completion was made and all was good – *very* good according to Genesis 1:31. Genesis 2:2 says, *"Thus the heavens and the earth were completed, and all their hosts."* The Hebrew word for "hosts" is '*Tsâbâ*' which includes 'everything in creation.' By the seventh day, all that would be made, was made - then He rested.

But wait a minute! For those of us who are detail finders, your red flag is probably waving frantically. This was declared by God *before* the creation of *Ishshah* – the woman! If God, who cannot lie, stated that every- thing that would be created *was* created by the end of the sixth day and He was very pleased with it, how could He announce creation's conclusion before the introduction of Adam's counterpart?

Confusion may stem from our inability to fully understand the implication of Genesis 1:26-27 wherein He said, "...Let Us make man in Our image, according to Our likeness; and let *them* rule ... and God created man in His own image, in the image of God He created him; male *and* female He created *them*." Just as God pulled His likeness from within Himself, and fashioned the human with His own qualities, the woman was *within* the man from the beginning! It's a mystery almost beyond human comprehension, but *we* – male and female – were *within* God from the very beginning! God tells the prophet Jeremiah, "Before I formed you in the womb, I *knew* you[10]." This word "knew" is the Hebrew word, "*yada*" which is a beautiful term for complete sharing – intimately knowing. We were in His thoughts, His imagination, and we were His longing way before the foundation of the world! He loved us before He formed our human- ness; we were a significant part of His makeup and circle of relationship. He knew who we were because we were a part of Him. Each one of us exhibit unique characteristics of our Father's likeness and each one of us is loved uniquely by the One who birthed and breathed life into us!

This same type of '*yada*' knowing is available between male and female - for the woman was *inside* of man when he was formed. She was *inside* of him when he could find no one like himself. Her presence *in* him very possibly intensified his deep longing for that 'one equal to or like unto him'! He *knew* somewhere deep down inside of him that there was some- thing more – or to be more exact – *someone like*. There was something inside that told him this adventure called 'life' is to be shared. In the quiet times, the longing for love to be given as well as received, flowed from the one inside who longed to make herself known. All said – when none could be found like him – Adam was *desperate* for he *knew* "It" was bigger than just him!

Therefore, when the woman was presented to him, I can almost hear him in a later conversation with Father...

---

[10] Jeremiah 1:5

"I knew it! I knew it! I knew there *had* to be another like me! Yet, to be so like me – she is also so different. She emanates life wherever she is. Even the tone of her voice is like a wonderful melody!"

"So, you are pleased with her?" Father smiled broadly.

"Pleased? There is no word that can fully describe my happiness. The only word that comes close to expressing what I feel is … complete. That's it! She *completes* me! In areas that I am weak – she, surprisingly, is strong! Where I lack, she has. But Father, it's much more than that. I still haven't fully figured it out. Somehow, I feel a completion beyond just complementary traits. It's like a 'circle of completion'. She once was *inside* me and now, in response to my love, she *receives,* and I move inside of her! When that happens, I feel totally *one* with her … completed!"

"Then, it is good!" Father laughed and gave Adam a big strong hug. "Go tell *Ishshah* that I look forward to hearing about her adventures this evening."

For me, life has been the ultimate adventure! I grew up in Alaska. I helped my uncle and grandparents tend to nearly fifty sled dogs and even learned to dog sled race! I grew up snow-skiing, fishing, and camping.

Over the years, wherever I go, people ask me, "What was it like living in Alaska?" Unless you have lived there, it is almost indescribable. However, I've developed a short response. It simply goes, "It's like living life consistently on the edge." It is knowing that your life may end at any moment, so you live life to the fullest. Earthquakes come … sometimes violently and always unannounced. Around the next corner may be a blizzard, bear or moose – and, for those who didn't know, moose are temperamental creatures that will kill you quicker than any bear.

Everything in Alaska is rugged; the mountains, the climate, and the men. Adventure for Alaskans is the balance between life and death. I've stood on tall mountaintops and looked at ... forever ... knowing that I may have very well been the *first* person to have stood at that earthen spot. That is adventure!

In the past, when I considered the Garden of Eden, unconsciously my mind conjured up the image of a dome-like bio-sphere-type structure enclosing a lush garden, climate controlled – an ecologist's paradise – but limited exploration. For this Alaskan, I couldn't help but picture Adam and Eve running into a glass boundary at some point.

It took a great deal of study and gleaning from other people before I could fully realize the great adventure these two set out on! First of all, they ventured out as emotionally healthy people with the ability to look outside of themselves instead of inwardly in an effort to fill emotional voids. One of the first things they received from their Father was a blessing![11] How many of us live our entire lives in search of our father's blessing? My husband was thirty-eight years old before he heard his father say, "Son, I am proud of you." The little boy in my strong husband melted.

A father's blessing will carve the course of life for their children. When it is withheld or the father is absent, the offspring will usually spend their entire lives finding alternatives to the real thing. A father's love and affirmation have a direct correlation to his daughter's fidelity. If a young girl interprets fatherly rejection, she will search for it in the arms of any man who will tell her what she most wants to hear – that she is loved[12]. In the case of sons, they usually seek power, prestige, or position to impress others in their effort to fill that large hole in their hearts.

When an emotionally healthy couple unites, they have the ability to minister 'to' rather than pull 'from' the other; thereby, avoiding the

---

[11] Genesis 1:28 "God blessed them; and God said to them, 'Be fruitful and multiply, and fill the earth, and subdue it; and rule over the fish of the sea and over the birds of the sky and over every living thing that moves on the earth."

[12] If you are interested in this subject, a good start would be an article by Julie Vaughan; Focus on the Family; 2010. http://www.focusonthefamily.ca/parenting/fatherhood/dads- and-the-daughters-they-love

unrealistic expectation that their happiness depends on their partner. Adam and Eve, it seems, were free from the emotional baggage that we tend to haul around and they set out uninhibited to the unexplored corners of their world. It helps me to think of the Garden as their "base of operation." After all, the whole world was there – just waiting for them. Did Adam show his fellow adventurer the wilderness where he was born? Did he help her scale the high mountaintop? Did they stand triumphantly at the top and survey 'forever' knowing that they were the first humans to set foot on that tall place?

Their divine charge was also a *joint* commission; as recorded in Genesis 1:28: "And God blessed *them*; and God said to *them*, 'Be fruitful and multiply, and fill the earth, and subdue it; and rule over the fish of the sea and over the birds of the sky, and over every living thing that moves on the earth."

Note that the man did not leave the woman home in the kitchen or with all the kids while he went off to have fun exploring. He knew that the Lord intended for life to be a joint adventure; something shared with 'one equal to or like unto to'. The woman's 'lot' in life was *not* relegated to sweeping out their living space with a straw broom and spending the days bent over a rock stove cooking mush for the man. No! She was commissioned right along with the man for the grand adventure!

Being an outdoors gal, I can envision the first man and woman floating down one of the four rivers on a makeshift hollowed log. Eve, a bit navigationally challenged, allows Adam to steer them along the fertile riverbanks as she lazily leans back and lets her foot drag through the water. Shielding her eyes with her hand, she gazes at the passing countryside, taking in all the sounds as they quietly drift by. Occasionally, they would pass a particularly beautiful shrub or tree, and she would take in the flowery aroma and ask Adam what the name of this or that one was. Then, without warning, she smelled a familiar scent. "Phew! I smelled that!"

With his back to her, a big smile broke loose, and he innocently replied, "What?"

"You tried to sneak that one out, didn't you? At least do that when I'm upwind from you!"

Adam tried hard to hold back his laugh, but the more he thought about it, the harder it was for him to keep from laughing. Before he knew it, he was doubled over in hysterics.

The woman, getting tickled by this time, repositioned herself then swung hard at the water, splashing the man with cold spray clear down his backside. This only made him laugh harder.

She smiled and leaned back again. She didn't know if she could love him any more than she did now. He made her laugh. He delighted in her. He loved her. Somehow, he reminded her of Father and she contemplated the enormity of her world - all of "it".

Their Name was Adam…
CHAPTER FIVE

"This is the book of the generations of Adam.

In the day that God created man, in the likeness of God made he him;
male and female created he them; and blessed them,

and called their name Adam (man),
in the day when they were created."

Genesis 5:1-2 (NASB)

"In the day that God created man…," He strategically hid the woman inside of him. I wonder if part of Adam's desperation came from the fact that he knew from his conversations with God that creation was completed - done. All that would *be* created, *was* created by the end of the sixth day. So, when the man could not find one equal to or like unto him, he probably thought there was no hope. Perhaps it crossed his mind that being alone may just be his 'lot' in life.

Still … he could not shake the inner voice that kept whispering to him, *"I am here. Keep looking. We were created for each other. Don't give up…"*

So, she waited. The word "wait" in Hebrew is "*qavah*". It means to gather together in oneness; to be bound together. In Genesis 1:9 where the Lord said, "Let the waters under the heavens be gathered together into one place, and let the dry land appear." That describes the word '*qavah*' or wait – it expresses an intertwining, much like strands of a rope that become one. So, *within* the man, she waited.

Meanwhile the man waited, looked, and did what he knew to do – work. Wilt Chamberlain once made a remark, "I believe good things come to those who work." If this is not in the Bible, it needs to be! Many (if not all) great leaders in the scriptures were called when they were "on the job" – Abraham in his father's shop, Moses tending sheep, David tending sheep, Gideon threshing wheat, and all the disciples in their trades. These were not lazy or indecisive men. They had purpose and direction.

The same was true with Adam. Before God brought the woman into his life, Adam was trained, ready, and more importantly, he had a viable, living relationship with the Lord! Relationships take time, they just don't happen overnight. It takes time to trust, to learn *who* the other one is, and to establish boundaries. I have friends whom I love very much, and we can spend hours talking about everything under the sun – except politics. Because I have spent *time* with these people, I know through experience that we just don't talk about certain things. Does a boundary diminish my love for these people? Of course not! I *know* them by spending time with them.

The time Adam spent with God was quality time, a Father training His son. Although I fully believe that Adam was created intelligent, he was not knowledgeable. He had to learn skills, facts, and proficiency in his job as Cultivator, Keeper, and Namer-of-animals. I am sure that their evening conversations were not surface yak, yak, yak – but deep learning sessions. I don't know about you, but just one word from God sustains *me* for months! I can only imagine bending His ear for hours!

Along with gaining knowledge about the earth and its abundance, I am sure Adam discovered who he was, and most importantly, who God was. In those one-on-one times with the Lord, I can hear some of Adam's questions and only ascertain the depth of Father's answers...

"Father?"

"What is it, My beloved?"

"Why is it that when I lay my head down at night, the area above brings forth lights – sometimes, so bright that I must find a large leaf to cover my eyes in order to sleep?"

"I made them. Don't you find them fascinating?"

"I find them most fascinating. In fact, some nights they seem so close that I could reach out and touch the lights! What do you call them?"

"They are called 'stars' and the expanse of them is called the heavens."

"I notice they stay in the same positions. But the big one – that real big one – changes. Every so often, some nights are extremely dark because it has disappeared completely! Is that a star as well?"

Father laughed. "No, son. That one is called the moon. Once you learn its patterns, you will be able to plant by it, reap by it, and even tend to animals by it."

"Is it one pattern or many patterns that I must learn?"

"Just one – but that one affects many things on this earth. There are many things that you will have to learn through experience; as I don't want to take the joy of discovery from you."

They were coming to the end of their walk that evening. Adam, like always, had a million questions – so he persisted with Father to sit and talk just a bit more. With a sigh, Father sat facing Adam and they rested against neighboring tree trunks.

"What about the stars? What is the purpose of them?"

"The stars? Well…what can I tell you about the stars? First of all, I put them in the heavens for signs and one day the culmination of these signs will convey a message. For your information, they do change and shift, but it takes centuries to notice any significance. Hidden in the mass of stars are constellations that tell an exciting story of a mortal conflict, an antagonist that seeks destruction, and a hero that redeems mortal man."[13]

"Really?"

"Would I lie to you?" God smiled.

Adam searched the darkening sky and knew their time together was coming to a close. "Father?"

"Yes, son?"

"Where might I find this hero hidden in the heavens?"

"Look deep within, Son. Look deep within." Father leaned over, kissed Adam on the forehead, then He was gone.

Adam, fighting grogginess, thought to himself, "*I will stay up tonight and see if I can locate that hero. It must be one of Father's mysteries that He wishes me to find...*" Within minutes, though, the song of the whippoorwill and the drone of the frogs lulled him into a deep sleep.

Father's story, however, had stirred his unconscious spirit. For his dreams conjured up nameless images of many humans held in bondage by a fiendish creature. They cried to God, who now was hidden from their eyes. Adam heard their cries – the sound of which he had never heard – and it tore at his heart. He broke out in a sweat and tossed his head back and forth. *Where was this hero? Who would save these humans?*

Just when all seemed hopeless, a figure appeared from the heavens. He looked much like Adam, a man – yet light radiated from him like God. He was riding upon a mighty white stallion, and a great host filled the sky behind him. He heard a loud cry coming up from the humans as they recognized this hero! Adam jerked and woke himself up. *They cried his name! What was his name? Remember Adam! What was this hero's name?*

---

[13] *The Real Meaning of the Zodiac*, Dr. James Kennedy, Ph.D. ©1989 Coral Ridge Ministries. Pg. 149. Summary

Try as he might, he could not recall the name he heard within his dream. If only he could meet this hero; this man-god. There was something *within* him that already knew and loved this being. And stranger still, he loved those people! Who were they? After all, it was only him. Adam sighed.

Now that he was awake, he lay and searched the star-filled sky and thought a lot about heroes.

When Adam was introduced to the woman, the hero inside came to life. Something in him *wanted* to be *her* hero. He wanted to protect her from any harm. He patiently taught her about which plants to avoid, what sinkholes looked like, and which animals were temperamental. He showed off his strength by lifting heavy logs out of her way and carrying her through the river rapids. At night he would envelope her in his arms securely, feeling like he just wanted to crawl inside her and she within him. He loved it when she would playfully squeeze his biceps and comment on how strong he was. In those moments, he was *the* man!

He was, after all, made in the image of God. The more time he spent with his Father, the more he recognized himself. With each passing day, he noticed certain mannerisms that mimicked his Creator; like the way he doted on the woman – protecting her from harm, the way he culti- vated her with his words of encouragement, how he went out of his way to provide for her, and the way he would talk of their future together and all the adventures they would have. These were all the Father's attributes! Yet, there was more to God than just these characteristics.

He spent the next few days studying the traits of each individual and making mental notes. When he thought he had it all figured out, he brought it up on that evening's walk.

"Father?"

"Yes, son?"

"Remember the first night you presented *Ishshah* to me?"

Father laughed! "How could I forget! I wouldn't trade that look on your face for anything! And the way you scampered back against that tree! I thought your eyes were going to pop out of your head..."

"Okay. Okay. You remember."

Muffling His laughter, Father responded, "Of course, I remember!"

Adam, turning a bit red in front of the woman, said, "Well, I couldn't help but notice that you called us both *adam* – man."

"Yes, I did."

"And it was I who called her *Ishshah* because she was taken out of Ish – man."

"Yes, you did."

"I know from studying, classifying, and naming the animals that although we have some things in common – *Ishshah* and I are not like them. We are a separate species."

"That is true." Father replied.

Ishshah rubbed up against Adam and made purring noises in his ear. "You know, my Adam, I *do* so like the lioness. She looks so wise and regal. Don't you think I am a lot like her?" And she smiled her beautiful smile at him.

He returned the smile, then reached out and pulled her in close. With his other hand, he messed up her hair and gave her a big squeeze. "No, I think you are more like the monkeys – swinging from trees and messing with me!"

Giggling, she shoved him, and he stumbled to the side a couple of steps. When he recovered, he joined the walk next to her. After a few steps, he bumped her with his hip – knocking her gently off the path. Laughing, she announced, "I *am* like a lioness!" Then, she regally regained her posture and walked next to him innocently. When the opportunity arose, though, on a slight incline - she bumped him. This play continued until they noticed Father was no longer near them; He had stopped a ways back and was watching the two play. It gave Him great joy to watch them.

Adam turned and said, "I'm sorry, Father! Stay there and we'll come join you – there is something I still want to ask you."

When they were all comfortable sitting on the side of a hill watching the sun begin to set, Adam continued his questioning. Glancing at the woman, he started, "As we concluded … we are NOT like the animals." She smiled. "We are a separate species. However, when I look into water's reflection or even at the woman, I see that we are like You. We even act like You!"

"And your question is?"

"Well," said Adam, "I notice that as a man, I tend to be like You in that I *want* to provide for the woman. I feel the need to protect her and build her up, encouraging her to new heights. However, I notice certain things about the woman - things that I don't necessarily possess – that are uniquely You as well."

"And what have you observed about her?'

"For one thing, her emotions are more overt than mine. She cries when she's happy, which I don't understand at all, and she laughs at the silliest things. She talks way more than I do, but most of all, she loves to be desired and told she is beautiful."

"And when you tell her she is wonderful, and worth being loved?" Adam smiled broadly, "Well…she *responds*!"

Ishshah leaned over, wrapped her arms around Adam's neck, and kissed him on the cheek.

Adam looked at Father and said, "See?"

They all laughed. For a brief moment they were quiet, all watching the sun begin its descent over the horizon. Adam searched his thoughts, trying to formulate the question that had been nagging at him. Finally, he started, "Father, what I've been trying to figure out is … well … it's almost too hard to put together rationally unless I tell you about the dream I had after our discussion about the stars and the mysterious story that the con- stellations tell of the hero…" Adam then shared his dream with them and how he knew this hero was a man-god. "But even more than that, I have *felt* that I already know this person who is much like You – just as when I was so desperate for my counterpart. Without knowing it in my head, my heart *knew* she was there – *inside*. Therefore, my question is two-fold. First, since we both portray your attributes – so uniquely, yet so completely – were we inside of you? And secondly, is this hero in me, as was the woman?"

Father thought for a moment. What could He tell the man without ruining the joy of discovery or revealing mysteries that are reserved for another age? Gazing out at the beautiful landscape and setting sun, Father asked, "Son, see all this?"

"Yes, it's beautiful."

"Thank you. It was in Me from the beginning. I saw its beauty *before*

I made it."

"And us?"

"You, too. I *knew* you before I fashioned you into human vessels. You were – and are – part of Me."

"And the hero?"

"Is within Us as well."

There was a moment of silence as the sun bid good night to their world. Then, Father spoke before departing, "As for the mystery, 'It' is bigger than this moment. However, you may begin by studying this seed." And God handed him the tiniest of seeds, kissed them both, then was gone.

Adam held that little seed all night. If only he knew that it would take generations upon generations of offspring before the world would know that Jesus, Yeshua Messiah, the ultimate hero, the One who saves us – was *inside* Adam at that moment, in his seed. "It" was much more than he could comprehend at that moment in time.

A Matter of Trust …

CHAPTER SIX

"And the Lord God commanded the man, saying,
"From any tree of the garden you may eat freely;
but from the tree of the knowledge of good and evil
you shall not eat,

for in the day that you eat from it you shall surely die."

Genesis 2:16-17 (NASB)

As stated in chapter two, God knew that the first humans would sin. He had already initiated a redemption plan for 'the day that [they ate] from it'. The boundary wasn't created to see if man was going to be obedient. The issue was never about obedience – but **trust**. If it was obedience that God required for relationship, He would have been very clear with the repercussions of the act of disobedience. He would have clearly laid out the consequences of noncompliance. He could have told them that it would introduce sin and its cohort, iniquity (the residue of sin); which would result in separation, disease, pain, and relational breakdown – not only to the ones who committed such an act, but to their children. Father could have stressed that the results of one bite from the fruit of *that* tree would result in the whole human race becoming a slave to death. Such an act of disobedience would affect all of mankind for thousands upon thousands of years!

As a mother, it was important to me that my boys didn't cross the line and engage in premarital sex. Since they were only a year apart in age, I sat them both down when they were give-or-take eleven and twelve years old. I told them that one day they would find themselves in the company of a girl who would make them feel as though they were God's gift to women! And that girl will whisper things in his ear that will make him tingle clear from the top of his head to the tip of his toes. And when that girl puts her hand on his thigh, it's going to feel as though he's about ready to crawl out of his skin, and when that happens … RUN! She has things you don't want! RUN!

Many years later, they remember *this* talk over my 'serious' version in which I clearly described the implications of unprotected premarital sex; pregnancy, sexually transmitted diseases, and emotional wounds. They didn't quite understand the emotional wounding part of it and may never will. However, from a woman's perspective there are often emotional wounds as an aftermath of premarital sex.

I'll never forget a ladies retreat I was at a few years ago. I don't recall the man's name who was speaking, but I'll never forget what he said. Veering from his outline, he said he felt led by the Holy Spirit to share an experience. In his past, he had taken advantage of a young gal who didn't necessarily want to have sex, but in his drunken stupor, he ignored her requests to stop. When all was said and done, he went on with his life. She, on the other hand, was emotionally stunted. She felt devalued, robbed, used, and very, very angry. She carried this around from relationship to relationship – never quite getting over it. Some twenty years later, they bump into one another. He responded to her like *nothing* ever happened and treated her like an old friend. She, however, seethed. Twenty years of vile anger and hatred shot from her eyes and poured from her mouth. It had never occurred to this man that this woman was still carrying that momentary act around. He took her by the shoulders, looked her square in the face, and said, "I am sorry." With that, she broke.

I looked around the room filled with ladies and watched their faces as they listened to this man's story. Many sat with clenched fists and defi- ant looks that held back their own haunting memories. Then this man did something that I wish every man who took advantage of a woman out- side the bounds of marriage would do. He said, "Ladies, as hard as this is to comprehend, hear me well. Sex to a man means ... nothing. Inside of marriage, however, it means *everything*. Outside, it is nothing but an act. But God used one woman to show me that to her it meant *something*. So, I stand up here as one man – but I represent all men – and I want to tell you, I'm sorry. I am truly sorry."

It took a moment for those words to sink in. But, one by one (me included) nearly every woman in that place wept! Tears poured like tor- rential rain from the deep places in their hearts, healing tears. Years of emotional hurt poured out. I have never seen so much healing take place! Those women were transformed by the apology of one man who had the courage to stand in the gap and take the blame of many men.

Was I able to communicate the full repercussions of pre-marital sex to my boys? Could I even begin to tell them of the emotional damage that many ladies carry around with them? I tried. I told them that before they even consider 'going there' to ask themselves – could this be my future wife? If not, it is somebody's future wife; and how would you like some guy to take advantage of your future wife? Furthermore, remember that she is somebody's daughter, somebody's sister – so **value** her! She really *wants* to be an eight-cow woman!

Did they listen? Not really. Like the first humans, they did what felt right at the moment; not considering ramifications or future consequences. Having said that, not many years after my "birds & bees" talk, we have a beautiful grand-daughter, Eliza, whom we don't get to see too often, but we pray for her all the time!

Will the young mother of our grand-daughter struggle with trust? Probably.

TRUST is the foundation of **every** healthy relationship. It is fruit of knowing you are loved – truly loved. But true love has a price far beyond what many are willing to pay. In his book, "The Shack", William Young states, "Love always leaves a significant mark."[14] In other words, love hurts. It hurts when we dare to trust in a relationship and become *vulnerable* – placing our hearts unprotected on a shared altar in the hope that it won't be smashed and broken into a thousand little humpty-dumpty pieces.

Love can also be spelled: **TIME**. My husband stood in front of a very "religious" audience one day and talked about the importance of us spending TIME with those we *say* we love. These people *said* they loved God and even memorized many scripture verses – though mostly, I think, to pass judgment and beat people up with. They learned the language of "Christian-eze" and went around calling each other "Brother" this and "Sister" that. They *said* to my husband, "I love you Brother Jesse." But this bothered my husband. He said to them that day:

"I have a brother named Gary. Now, when I call my brother, I don't tell him – Hi Brother Gary. No! I *know* he's my brother. Why? Because we have spent TIME together. We may have our spats, but I know he will always be my brother. You *say* you love me, and you *say* you love God. If that is so, let me ask you some questions…

▶ What is my favorite color?

▶ What things in life do I like or dislike?

▶ What about the personality of Jesus?

---

[14] Young, William P., "The Shack", 2007, Windblown Media, Newbury Park, CA, chapter 6

▶ What is He like?

▶ What does He smell like?

If you don't know the answer to these questions, you have NOT invested TIME into the relationship. For those who just can't wait – or don't have the TIME – I like the color green, I like the outdoors but hate snakes and sharks. And Jesus? You will just have to spend TIME to get to know Him – but He does smell like brokenness (which my wife insists smells like frankincense and French toast)."

The cost of love is vulnerability and TIME. The fruit from this investment in another being is TRUST. What a sweet thing when both parties involved can be trusted! I heard a live worship recording with Derick Webb (formerly associated with the music group Caedman's Call) and he talked about how he secretly wished that God would just take his life and preview it up on a great big screen so that all of mankind could see his deepest, darkest, bad-est, most sinful moments. That way, he could repent, and everyone could deal with it all in one moment's time. He wanted to become totally vulnerable to be totally set free! No more judgment. No more time and effort spent trying to make himself look good. No more walls between him and God and him and others – just living real with God, real with himself, and real with others.

I thought to myself, *"Wow. I want that kind of freedom and trust in relationship. Lord, You can do that with me if you want. I just want REAL."*

Oh, my Good Lord Jesus! What occurred shortly after that heart- talk with God was one of the most painful experiences of my and Jesse's life! The moment you decide to totally trust God with the key to all your locked-up, rarely-visited, deep dark chambers of your innermost being – the enemy will take that vulnerable heart just sitting there on the altar and crush the smithereens out of it! In chapter three, we discussed that we need to know our enemy. Satan does not want us to be *real* in relationship. He operates in the shadows of distrust. Therefore, within moments of my declaration, he set to work in the congregation of people... sowing distrust.

What resulted in a very short time was a small, but powerful little group of people (claiming to be Christians) that found offense with us. The ringleader, a lady who wanted to be the "spiritual guru" of the Church, became jealous when her husband was being raised up in leadership. She secretly filmed him in a display of rage and anger at home – all of which she provoked. She brought the film to my husband, Jesse, who refused to watch it. He was appalled that she provoked her husband for the sake of bringing him down. After not getting her way, she left and started pulling in others who now found common purpose. Together, they began a frenzied attack to discredit and run us out of town. They perused the internet, they used law enforcement to perform illegal background searches on us, they called former churches where we served, they called former business associates, they called our Bishops, they even went back thirty-five years and called my high school reunion group! In the community and to the members of our church, lies were told about us, false witness was sworn about us, they took half-truths and turned them into un-truths about us. They tried to get me fired from my job. They tried to have our pastoral credentials stripped from us. We were dumb-founded, shell-shocked, and angry!

Wherever I went, at home, at work, in my car, and even in the Church, I prayed much like David had at times ... "Lord! In Your loving-kindness, justice, and ever-lasting goodness – JUST RIP THEIR LIPS OFF!!!" I really trusted that my Abba Daddy would be as appalled at these "pharasitical piranhas" as I was. They were operating in the same spirit as those who hunted down Jesus.

My trust waivered as Daddy did... nothing. I failed to see His good-ness at work in the midst of all the darkness. Six months passed. By this time, the attacks were so severe (and public) that our Bishop had to be called in. When he arrived, the word from the enemy camp was that this was going to be our "De-Frock" Sunday – the day in which we would be tarred, feathered, and run out of town.

That Sunday morning, the sanctuary was packed out. To our wonderful surprise, townspeople – the un-churched with whom we had been building relationship with – showed up and locked arms with those who faithfully stood with us throughout this ugly ordeal. The powerful little group of attackers sat crowded at the back. By the time Bishop Ray Willis was done speaking, seven people gave their heart to the Lord and the attackers hurriedly exited the building. Throughout the following year and a half, there were eight more salvations and eighteen baptisms! More than the whole twenty-year history of that little church! I repented for doubting His goodness in ALL situations.

What I like even more is the freedom I now walk in. Along with the miracle of lives being saved, I am grateful that God changed *my* heart as well. I no longer petition for Him to "rip their lips off"; but I pray, for their own sakes, that they have that REAL encounter with Jesus. If they really knew Him and spent TIME with Him, they would know He does not delight in murdering other people through gossip, tale bearing, and deflecting their own guilt upon others.

> *TRUST in the Lord with all your heart, Lean*
> *not on your own understanding.*

Proverbs 3:5

I have heard it said that "Faith is not belief without proof but rather trust without reservation."[15] It reminds me of the story about the un-named 'woman with an issue' in Mark 6:25-34. She comes on the scene and is introduced as the woman with a problem. For twelve years, everyone in her community knows her as the "woman with an issue". Worse yet, cultural paradigms marked her as the UNCLEAN woman; and her community dutifully ostracized her. She might as well be walking around with a large scarlet letter "U" embroidered on her tunic. She has lost her identity,

---

[15] David Elton Trueblood (1900 - 1994), noted 20th century American Quaker author and theologian, former chaplain both to Harvard and Stanford universities.

her friends, her family, her money, and endured *much* at the hands of many practicing physicians. As a side note, how many of us today have suffered at the hands of those *practicing* religion? They put on a good show, say all the "right" prayers – but, then blame *you* when nothing happens. Some even add more grief to an already bad situation by telling us that it was because of *our* lack of faith that we were not healed. The truth is God simply refused to perform when *they* commanded Him to do so! Their motives would have stolen the Glory from God, who is Sovereign. The woman in this story, like so many of us, doesn't have a lack of faith – she just hasn't found the answer!

Romans 10:17 says, *"Faith comes by hearing and hearing by the word of Christ."* This un-named woman heard the gospel (the good news) about Christ and the Word says she targeted in on Truth; trusting with all her heart that if she could just touch the tzitzit of his outer garment she would be made well. Wow! That is a woman trusting without reservation! As the story went, she pressed her way through the crowd, touched the Master's garment, and was immediately healed! But then, the unthinkable happens... she is caught!

I can only imagine her mind racing with old lies; *"you're unclean"*; *"you're not supposed to be anywhere near people"*; *"something is wrong with you"*; *"you did something to cause this illness"*; *"you are a nobody"*. Yet here before her, stood Truth ... there He was ... the Son of God!

I love what this gutsy lady did. Even though she was afraid, she still came and fell at the feet of Jesus and "told Him the WHOLE TRUTH[16]". She came clean with Christ – got REAL before Him! She trusted Him enough to tell Him the truth. It was this trust without reservation that brought about her health. Furthermore, instead of her identity being that of a woman with a problem, Jesus redeemed her identity and value by calling her "Daughter". Finally, he restored her eternal worth, for her story has been told throughout the generations!

---

[16] Mark 5:33

Trust is a big issue with God. He talks a lot about it through His Word. Not only does He want us to trust *Him*, but He wants to be able to trust *us*. Some read the Word and ascertain that it is all about commandments and our need to be obedient to the Law. However, I read the Word and I see covenants of love and His wanting us to just TRUST Him – fully knowing who we are and whose we are!

I wonder if Adam and Eve understood "it" was a "trust issue" with Father, not just a boundary…

Part One of "The Turning" ...
CHAPTER SEVEN

———————◦———————

"And those who know Your name
Will put their trust in You,

For You, O'Lord

Have not forsaken those who seek You.

Psalm 9:10

Our whole walk with God is a trust issue. Real trust can only exist and thrive in a relationship where we are free to reject it. Within the lush garden, God placed a forbidden fruit, the Tree of Knowledge of Good and Evil. We know from the Word that "God is Good" and Evil (*Ra'* in Hebrew) is everything that operates apart from God who is Good. Rather than hide this Tree in some distant hidden part of the world, God placed it in the very center of their base of operation – allowing them a daily choice to just trust in His Goodness or choose to do what they wanted to do apart from Him. The root of sin is simply the desire to *do* things ourselves – apart from the will of God. The Tree wasn't a test of obedience or loyalty, it was a *trust* issue.

If we were truly honest with ourselves, there are many times in our lives that we really don't TRUST God and that He works "all things together for our good."[17] Like many others, for years I lived a contradictory life. On one hand I loved God, but on the other... I didn't trust Him. In my eyes, He had let me down – didn't live up to my expectations. When I needed Him most, He seemingly was not there. So, I lived life on *my* terms, doing what "I" thought was right; but in actuality, I was toting my baggage from one messy relationship to another.

After nearly two decades of doing this, I cried out in desperation to this God I loved - as well as harbored hatred for. I was at the end of my "self." I didn't know how to fix all the hurt the years had accumulated. There was no hiding behind the mask of perfection any longer; for the ugly root of bitterness seeped through the seams and affected those in relation- ship around me. Hurting people indeed hurt people.

That night I asked God to go to the very root of all the hurt and bitterness. In all sincerity, I told Him that I could not bear the pain of recalling even yesterday; therefore, how could I go back through the weeks, months, and years of hurt piled upon hurt? Allowing Him access to the locked-up, chained, and heavily guarded dark chambers of my heart was an act of trust. I determined myself, though, to trust Him.

In response to my willingness to wholeheartedly trust Him, God sent His son! In that dark bedroom, Jesus appeared next to the bed and asked me to grab hold of His hand, and He would take me to the pivotal moment in my life – the root of all my hurt. At that moment, there was nothing left to trust but Him, so I took hold of His hand.

Suddenly, what resembled a big movie screen opened before my eyes. I saw myself as a girl of fifteen lying sick on the sofa one afternoon.

Memories of that day, hidden and locked up in deep chambers, projected from my heart for all to see. I had stayed home from school that day nursing a cold; and as the scene unfolded before me, I watched my five-year- old little brother come in and play with his toy car garage. All was well until my stepfather, who was an alcoholic, entered the living

---

[17] Romans 8:28

room. I knew well the tell-tale signs of trouble; and as he started picking at my brother, I instinctively and very quietly gathered up my bedding, tip-toed to my bedroom, and hid under the covers. It was only moments before I heard his heavy footsteps march down the hallway. The bedroom door burst open and his six-foot three-inch; three-hundred pound frame filled the opening. His hollering was inconsequential – as I had already heard all the lies before..."*Who do you think you are?... You are nobody! ... You will never amount to anything!... How dare you cop that attitude with me!...*" It was the hitting that concerned me. I cowered further under the covers.

When he realized the blows were not hurting me, he threw back the covers and started pounding me with his big fists. In my head, I heard a voice say, "*Get up!*" I scrambled across the bed and planted my feet firmly on the floor – with nowhere to go as he was still blocking the doorway. I stood there facing him but not daring to say a word.

The next thing I knew, a big fist slammed me across the cheek and sent my little five foot-two-inch frame flying to the floor. I heard the voice again… "*Get up!*" So, I grabbed the side of the bed and pulled myself up. Once again, I stood before him. Another face shot and I was down. This played over and over until I could no longer get up.

Watching these scenes made me want to throw up. He had beat me up so bad that time that I could not go to school for the next two weeks. But that wasn't the worst of it. I quit talking. Finally, after weeks of a house filled with tension and silence, my mom (who was coping with all the dysfunction the best she knew how[18]) confronted me and said, "*I don't care how YOU fix this – but you need to fix it!*" I was made to apologize to the man who beat me for no reason. Unbeknown to us at the time, this mandate set me up for a lifetime of feeling as if I was the one at fault when men abuse me.

---

[18] Please note that I am not and never have blamed my mom for my problems. She is a beautiful strong lady, who like me, was trying to survive in not-so-good situations. By her example, I learned to hold my head up and act like a lady. I love and honor her as my mother and my friend.

Turning from the "screen", I glared at Jesus, who still held my hand, and angrily spat out the words, "I TRUSTED YOU! AS A 15-YEAR-OLD GIRL, I LOVED YOU AND TRUSTED YOU … YET YOU DID NOTHING!"

He looked at me compassionately and said, "Let Me show you what really happened that day." Then, with a wave of His hand, the scene re-wound and started over.

- ▶ I lie on the couch;
- ▶ In comes my dad who starts picking on my brother;
- ▶ I tip-toe to the bedroom;
- ▶ He bursts into my room and starts beating me;
- ▶ I hear the voice, "Get up!"…

Jesus interjected, "I was that voice. In this life, you will sustain blows – but you will face them standing up. You are a strong woman." I reminded Him, "You still didn't help me…"

He said, "Watch…"

- ▶ The blows continued again and again, until I could not get up anymore…

This time, however, as I gazed at the "screen" before me, there was an invisible *dome* surrounding both my dad and me during this episode. I asked Jesus what this was.

He responded, "It is 'parental authority'. We have given many rights to parents to raise up their children. Since your parents were not believers, I could not intervene. However, let Me show you what I did do…" And the scene re-wound again:

- ▶ I lie on the couch;

- ▶ In comes my dad who starts picking on my brother;

- ▶ I tip-toe to the bedroom;

- ▶ He bursts into my room and starts beating me;

- ▶ I hear the voice, "Get up!"

- ▶ My dad rears back to hit me…

I watched as his fist – in slow motion – came across my left cheek, throwing my head violently to the right and my little body across the room. However, as this was happening, I noticed that the body of Jesus which had been standing all this time with me – melded and became part of me on the screen. When the blow hit me, His head was thrown violently – together with mine – and we landed together on the floor. His arms and hands helped me to get back up. Then He stood again, melded with me, waiting for the next blow.

I stared at the scene – speechless. After a moment, He pulled my face toward His and said, "I NEVER left you. I felt EVERYTHING you did – all the pain, all the hurt – I took upon Myself. I never left you and I will never, ever leave you."

Years of pent-up hurt and perceived abandonment poured forth. I fell to my knees, wrapped my arms around His knees, and asked Him to forgive me for being angry with Him all these years. He knelt and held me for the longest time – rocking me as a Father would.

Then, He said, "I need to show you one more thing; as you are not without guilt in this matter."

Although surprised, I was not offended, for after repenting and seeing things through His eyes, I now trusted Him. So, the scene re-wound *again*…

- ▶ I lie on the couch;

- ▶ In comes my dad who starts picking on my brother;

- ▶ I tip-toe to the bedroom;

- ▶ He bursts into my room and starts beating me;

- ▶ I hear the voice, "Get up!"

- ▶ My dad rears back to hit me…

- ▶ Jesus helps me get up…

Having my eyes opened to reality – I now saw truth from God's perspective. In this scene, I watched as I dragged myself up from the floor again through His eyes. However, this time, my eyes locked-on to my dad as he readied himself to deliver another punch. Right before he swung, from my eyes shot a silver cord that wrapped around his body and back around mine.

Surprised, I looked at Jesus and asked Him what this was.

He responded, "It is judgment. You judged him that day and from then on out, he was bound to treat you in the same manner in which you judged him."

As soon as I uttered the words, "Please forgive me", the cord was broken. Not only did repentance set my dad free, but it enabled me to just be *me* with God. I now fully trust Him.

It took years, but my stepfather eventually made his peace with God and my heart grieved when he lost the battle to a long illness. Not only did I love and honor him, but I also had the distinct honor of officiating over his funeral.

When I was raising my boys, I expected them to trust me. Every decision I made was for their good because I loved them. I don't think parents should have to explain their every action to their children. Likewise, with God, we are often on a "need-to-know basis". Had God sat down on the couch with me that day and warned me that I was going to receive a horrific beating for no obvious reason, I would have taken matters into my own hands and plotted an alternate course of action for the remainder of the day! Although sick, I would have hidden in my closet or even left for a friend's house. This could have resulted in my becoming a coward, spiraling me into an avoidance pattern for the rest of my life. I am strong today because of what He allowed me to go through.

For our own sakes, God, our Father, wants us to trust His awesome love for us. When hardship comes, our first question should be, "Lord, what do you desire me to learn through this?' Then, courageously walk *through* the trial trusting in His goodness and knowing that He is there with you - feeling EVERYTHING you do and taking it all upon Himself. When you arrive on the other side of the problem, not only do you have a testimony, but hindsight is a valuable tool. Retrospect often brings the revelation of the "bigger picture".

Whatever you are going through, there is always something bigger going on than what you see and perceive – for 'it' matters to God how we get through it!

Part Two of "The Turning" …
CHAPTER EIGHT

———⌘———

"When the woman saw that the tree was good for food,
And that it was a delight to the eyes,

And that the tree was desirable to make one wise,
She took from its fruit and ate;

And she gave also to her husband with her,
And he ate.

Genesis 3:6 (NASB)

Trouble rarely makes a grand entry into our life. Rather, it sneaks up from behind and "sucker-punches" us when we least expect it. There were no red flags, alarms, or whistles of warning the day that "Nâchâsh", the hissing creature (that was also created by the hand of God), appeared by the forbidden tree in the Garden. By all accounts, that day – as all others – was a *normal* day in Paradise.

Adam and Eve's lack of surprise at this creature's appearance causes me to wonder if they were accustomed to his presence by this time. Had he hung around them and studied them long enough to know their individual weaknesses, as well as earn a degree of trust with them? Did he overhear hints of a secret longing for forbidden knowledge? Over time, did he plant seeds of doubt knowing that all disobedience flows from mistrust? Did he cause them to wonder *why* they could eat freely from any tree in the Garden but *that* one?

Why? … is the all-inclusive question. The answers to "who", "what", "when", and "where" are directly fact-driven and readily understood. There is nothing more to know about a situation until we consider the under-lying motivation – "Why?" When we ask this question, we infer that **we** know "what" is best and compel the recipient of this inquiry to justify their position; thereby questioning their trustworthiness and – ultimately – the depth of their love for us.

When God presented the Garden to Adam, giving him the import- ant task of cultivating and keeping it, He charged Adam to not eat "from the tree of the knowledge of good and evil … for in the day that you eat from it you shall surely die." I wonder if Adam took notice that God did not say "*if* you eat from it". God, who sees the timeline from the beginning to the end, and intimately knows us, knew that man would indeed eat from that tree.

At the time of this command from God, Eve was securely hidden within Adam. Somewhere along the way, Adam relayed this command to Eve. However, I'm almost sure that he added to Yahweh's mandate, a warn-ing to Eve, "…don't even touch it!" One thing I have learned about life is that when humans get involved, there is always a contradiction or a water-ing-down of truth. By adding to what God said, I can't help but wonder if Eve questioned why the squirrels, birds, and the serpent did not die by "touching" the tree. One can be so close to Truth yet miss it by miles.

Like the rolling of dice in a board game, "red-letter" days are bound to happen. It's the time when all the historical pieces fit together and our response to a given situation determines our future. Leading up to that "red-letter" moment in Paradise … all that had been said, learned, and shared could have culminated in a manner such as this…

On that historical day, Adam and Eve walked hand-in-hand together toward the Garden interior. After an early morning dip in the springs, they headed into the center for their breakfast of fruit from the Tree of Life and the surrounding foliage. As Eve worked her way around the side of The Tree to reach for some produce, she heard the sounds of one eating nearby. Out of the corner of her eye, she caught sight of Nâchâsh, the hissing creature. He was leaning against the forbidden tree holding up the succulent fruit that was dripping down his arm.

With one hand, he wiped his mouth while letting a pleasant "Yummmm" sound escape his lips. He looked at Eve and innocently asked, "Indeed, has God said, 'You shall not eat from every tree of the Garden'?"[19]

Eve, who had spoken often with this creature, responded to this challenge with, "From the fruit of the trees of the Garden we may eat; but from the fruit of the tree, which is in the middle of the Garden, God has said, 'You shall not eat from it, or *touch* it, lest you die[20].'"

The serpent cleverly pointed out that which is true to prove a point that is not, ultimately driving a wedge further between God and these people. He held out the half-eaten fruit and retorted, "You surely shall not die![21]"

The proof was there. Not only had he *touched* the tree, but he was eating of its fruit – and nothing happened. No lightning from heaven. He didn't croak or melt into a smoldering pile. But rather, he stood there bliss- fully enjoying every juicy bite!

Then, as man so often does, Nâchâsh projects his own guilt upon the vulnerability of another. Cunningly, he hissed softly, "…For God knows that in the day you eat from it your eyes will be opened, and you will be

---

[19] Genesis 3:1 – New American Standard Bible
[20] Genesis 3:3 – New American Standard Bible
[21] Genesis 3:4 - New American Standard Bible

like God, knowing good and evil[22]." Not only was this the very thing that caused his [Lucifer's] removal from heaven, but he manipulatively insinuated that God could not be trusted. One would think from this statement that God, in His insecurity, would be threatened if anyone else were *like* Him – knowing good and evil.

However, here before their eyes was a living creature that was wise in the ways of good and evil. Obviously, he knew something that they did not. We often take on the character of those whom we let speak into our life. Rather than Eve turn to Adam and say, "Honey, this doesn't line up with what you told me – and I don't think something is right here.", she chose to trust in what she saw and what she thought best. I can only imagine how that day would have played out had she known God well enough to trust in His love for her!

The Word says that the forbidden tree was "*desirable* to make one wise[23]..." This word, desirable is "*Châmad*" which means, to desire, to covet, to long for. Is it wrong for one to want to be wise? She longed for a good thing. After all, wouldn't it be great to have long intelligent talks with God who is all-wise?

Sadly, though, there are many who desire good things, then "spiritualize" them by rationalizing that having certain things, gifts, or talents will somehow bring them to a "higher" level with God.

"If only I could preach like..."

"If only people would fall or be healed when I prayed for them..."

"If only I could deliver a revelation word from God...that would validate me as a Prophet..."

"If only I could reach a level with God that nobody else has..."

---

[22] Genesis 3:5 – It is interesting to note that the serpent (representing Satan) projected the very same thing he is guilty of, that is, wanting to be like God. Those who are guilty do not want to go down alone – they take everyone else with them!

[23] Genesis 3:6 – New American Standard Bible

All of these desires are "Luciferian" in nature. He wanted to be *like* God – above the rest. The focus is on "I" and what "I" can obtain. The rhetoric taking place at the base of the forbidden tree is the basis of evil (*ra'* – which is all that is apart from good). God, who is Good, reveals His heart about the sanctity of relationship through the writing of Paul in II Corinthians 11:2-3 (NASB):

> For I am jealous for you with a godly jealousy; for I betrothed you to one husband, that to Christ I might present you as a pure virgin. But I am afraid, lest as the serpent deceived Eve by his craftiness, your minds should be led astray from the *simplicity* and *purity of devotion* to Christ.

I can almost hear the deafening silence as all inhabitants of heaven hold their breath and creation stills itself for the moment of decision. I can see the serpent comfortably leaning against the stately tree and letting the sun glisten off the juicy fruit while he keeps his gaze locked with Eve's. He knew their weaknesses and was betting everything he had on this moment. He, the one banished from Love's presence, would take all of humanity with him to Judgment – ultimately turning the power of love upon Love itself.

As a spectator imagining this scene eons later, I am crying out to Eve, *"TURN EVE! TURN YOUR GAZE TO ADAM – HE WILL BE YOUR HERO IF YOU LET HIM!"* Then, I scream loudly to Adam, *"WAKE UP! GOD CREATED YOU TO BE THE HERO! NOW IS YOUR TIME, STEP UP TO THE PLATE AND BE THE MAN!"*

Sadly, they could not hear the warnings of millions of offspring seeded in their loins; and Eve reached out and took fruit from the tree ... and ate. Then, she gave some to her husband who was with her, and he ate. Nâchâsh flashed a smile at the two, took another juicy bite, and settled down into the lush grass to watch sin play out.

In their previous state of innocence and purity, they did not fully comprehend that sin – at its root – is simply grabbing for ourselves what God has not given to us.

Over the years I have heard this "red-letter" day referred to as the "Fall of Man" – likening it to when Lucifer fell from the heavens. In my opinion, this day should more appropriately be referred to as "The Choosing" or "The Turning".

In this fateful moment, mankind turned from totally trusting God to trusting in their own wisdom. Relationships are based upon trust. Even though God would have come in a nano-second, had they summoned Him, they trusted their own judgment. Without realizing "it", their declaration of independence impacted all of heaven and all of earth for all of eternity… but God knew "it" would happen…

Consequences
CHAPTER NINE

———————◦———————

"...Who told you that you were naked?

Have you eaten from the tree

Of which I commanded you not to eat?"

Genesis 3:11 (NASB)

When our son returned from overseas combat duty, his way of dealing with painful issues was to hang out with the guys, play poker, drink, and God knows what else, till the wee hours of morning (and sometimes all night). This behavior didn't sit well with Mama because I thought he should be spending time at home with his wife and child. Whenever he would stop by the house for a visit, I emphatically let him know what he was doing was wrong. It didn't take long before my judgmental attitude drove a BIG wedge between us.

As I sat on the patio steps one day pouring my heart out to God and lamenting over where our son was *at* instead of where he *should* be, He reminded me about *me*. The Holy Spirit said, "Do you remember when *you* were searching in all the wrong places for *your* Love, Acceptance, and Worth?"

Of course I did. Nobody screamed "SHAME" louder than I did. Nobody had to tell me that what I was doing was wrong because the "Knower" in me knew it. In those days of searching and messing it all up, I gravitated not toward my parent's house, but to my grandparents' home. Sitting around that little dining table snugly fitted in the kitchen, Grandma would put aside whatever she was doing and talk *with* me – not *at* me. She made me feel so valuable that it challenged me to rise above my shameful circumstances. Did she hand over volumes of carefully selected wise adages or advice? No. She just loved on me. Love is often spelled, TIME Like the spoken word, it is one of the few things we can never take back once it is given.

Humbled, I vowed from that day forward to be *that* kind of Mama to my boys. It took a little while, but it wasn't long before Matthew felt safe, and loved enough, to talk through his issues with us. Today, many years later, he and his wife are doing well, and he often calls me … just to talk.

There are no step-by-step plans, easy formulas, or magical incantations for navigating our way through trials or out of messes. It is our Father's way of honoring us. He has given us all we need to maneuver through the obstacles in life. What He offers us instead, is relationship! Like my grandma, He will spend that TIME and just love on us – that is, if we will come out of hiding and sit at His table.

What a difference a moment of time makes in our lives! In an instant, Adam and Eve withdrew from relationship with Father, claimed their independence, and now found themselves in hiding. The "Knower" within them *knew* they had royally messed up. Collaboratively, they sewed some fig leaves together to cover their nakedness and to hide their vulnerability from each other - and God.

Jerusalem, as recorded in Lamentations 1:8-9 (NASB), messed up as well:

Jerusalem sinned greatly. Therefore, she has become an unclean thing. All who honored her despise her because they have seen her nakedness; even she herself groans and turns away…. she did not consider her future [her destiny]…

An old friend of mine, Tom Belt, wrote about "The Sanctity of the Moment" in a social post a few years back. I don't recall what the rest of his discourse was, but those words resonated in my spirit. I was guilty of taking life's *moments* – each precious one – and squandering the value of it. I gave little thought to my every step being orchestrated by God. I flippantly raced by moments not realizing that each one of them determines not only *my* future [destiny], but that of others as well! Like so many of us, I don't think Adam and Eve fully considered the ramifications their rash decision would have on their future or that of their offspring.

Every one of our decisions results in consequences – good or bad. When the choice of a moment is sanctified, set apart for the will of God and His goodness, all is well. However, when the moment becomes about us and what we want, it leaves a mess. Iniquity is the messy residue of sin – the harsh consequences of operating apart from God's Goodness.

It is theologically incorrect to interpret what happened next in this Garden setting as "Judgment" or God "cursing mankind". So many of us have come to believe that at this point God stopped loving them, withdrew His presence, and is now seated in His judge's chambers holding a gavel in His hand … just *waiting* for us to screw up.

But rather, the Lord God who knows everything and still loved them passionately, put down what He was doing and gave them His entire attention! They knew He would beckon them to come spend TIME with Him and just be real with Him. I can't help but wonder what would have happened in that intimate setting if they threw themselves in Daddy's lap and whole-heartedly repented – each owning up to their actions. But we usually don't do that when we sin. We hide instead.

So, the Lord God beckoned, "Adam, where are you?[24]" The Lord knew where Adam was; but Adam needed to know where he was. Adam was created appositionally, he was friend with the Creator of the Universe, he was Cultivator & Keeper of the Garden, he was Namer-of-Animals, and husband to Eve – yet here he was cowering in the foliage. Furthermore, taking on the character of the one he allowed to speak into his life, he proceeded to deceive God by leading Him to believe that he was hiding *because* he was naked. At this point, when he was responding to God, Adam was not naked but already covered (with fig leaves).

The Lord God ignored this ugly residue of sin and zeroed in on the problem – which was allowing the wrong spirit to speak into his life. He said, *"Who told you* that you were naked?[25]" We need to guard what we receive from others because it is often easier to believe the lies than the truth about us. Even Jesus rebuked a good saying from a wrong spirit.[26]

Then God opened the door, inviting Adam to come to the table of truth. He said, "Have you eaten from the tree of which I commanded you not to eat?[27]" In an instant, Adam deflected responsibility and pointed toward his wife and said, *"That woman* whom *You* gave to be with me, *she* gave me from the tree, and I ate.[28]"

In a moment's time – all had changed. Without blinking an eye, Adam hastily sacrificed the one he adored, his partner in the adventure called *Life*, the flesh-of-his-flesh and bone-of-his-bone. I wonder how this scenario would have played out had Adam threw himself on the altar and willingly offered to sacrifice his life for hers that day?

---

[24] Genesis 3:9

[25] Genesis 3:11

[26] Matthew 16:23 "But He turned and said to Peter, 'Get behind Me, Satan! You are a stum- bling block to Me; for you are not setting your mind on God's interests, but man's.'" (NASB)

[27] Genesis 3:11

[28] Genesis 3:12

Then, adding insult to injury, Adam had the audacity to blame God! "*You* gave her to me, Lord![29]" Doing this, he inferred, "It's ultimately *Your* fault, not mine! ... when you made me, you made a good thing – but, when you made *her* ... she's defective."

Saddened, the Lord God looked at Eve. He didn't ask her "Why?" - which would compel her to justify *what* she did. But rather, He said to Eve, "*What* is this you have done?[30]" At first reading, one would think that Eve blamed the devil fully for her actions. However, the statement she makes is really one of confession. She states, "The serpent deceived me, and I ate.[31]" Yes, the devil played a role, but I fell for it.

Unfortunately, centuries of mankind have punished women because of Eve's single act. I find it hard to understand why mankind has focused blame on females for a "curse" when all God wanted was for both of the humans to fess up to what they did. The scriptures say that **Adam** is the one who affected all of mankind. Romans 5:19 (NASB) says, *"For as through the one man's disobedience the many were made sinners, even so through the obedience of the One the many will be made righteous."* Paul blames Adam, not Eve. Eve was deceived and admitted it – partly because she was given a watered-down version of God's commandment concerning the tree. Adam sinned with full recognition of what he was doing.

After Eve's confession, the Lord God turned to the serpent. It is interesting to note that God allowed Adam and Eve the honor of answering, But He gave no such honor to the serpent. Instead, He cursed the serpent and sentenced him to a life wallowing in the dust on his belly and whose seed will be avenged by the seed of the woman.[32]

To the woman He said, "I will greatly multiply your pain in childbirth, in pain you shall bring forth children."[33] She will now identify with

---

[29] Genesis 3:12
[30] Genesis 3:13
[31] Genesis 3:13
[32] Genesis 3:15
[33] Genesis 3:16

Father God who births forth a son into human form to take on Himself all the sins of mankind. She will identify with the pain Father endures witnessing His Son tortured and crucified for those whom He loves. Woman, who is representative of the Church, will travail in birth pangs for the coming King (Matthew 24:8, Mark 13:8).

Then, the Lord God prophesies over the woman. He tells her that her "*Tshûwqâh*", which means her 'turning', her 'desire', or her 'reaching out after' shall now be directed toward her husband. With the Lord God declaring it at this encounter, it implies that it is a *new* thing. Otherwise, why state it? Evidently, up to this point, her fulfillment was a result of her relationship with Father God. It was He who made her feel totally loved, accepted and approved of, as well as her worth derived exclusively from Him. Now, however, the consequence of her declaration of independence and distrust in God is that she will now expect her *husband* to fill the basic L.A.W. needs she has (i.e. to know that she is loved, accepted and approved of, and has worth).

Her husband's response to this expectation will be to rule over her. We tend to do that with the "needy" people in our life. When they hand over the obligation of our taking absolute care of them and the expectation that their happiness depends on us, it in essence, gives us the 'right' to lord over them. God did not intend for us to derive our worth from anyone else but Him. The benefit of intimately knowing who we are in Him, is that it frees us to be in healthy relationship with others! Eve was in healthy relationship with Adam until the moment she withdrew from healthy relationship with God.

Furthermore, this declaration from God to the woman, "Your desire will be toward your husband, but he will rule over you"[34], was an admonition for Adam to rise up and be the hero he was created to be. When we are set in authority over people, we are *responsible* for them. Authority =

---

[34] Complete Jewish Bible; 1998 by David H. Stern; Jewish New Testament Publications, Inc. Genesis [B'Resheet]

responsibility, not 'lording over'. Christ, our "head", does not dictate over us, but as our Savior, He saves us from ourselves. He is our Hero!

Before the woman was drawn out of Adam, God gave him jobs that would train him for how he was to relate to the one like him, but frailer. Adam was trained to be a cultivator, nurturer, and maintainer. The Garden didn't need to be beaten with plowshares, but developed, attended to, and worked with. Additionally, as Namer-of-Animals, Adam learned the importance of studying over something and speaking purpose over it. In a later chapter we will return to this subject when we learn how the husband is responsible for sanctifying his wife [setting her apart for God's purpose], having cleansed her by the washing of water with the *word*. (Eph. 5:26)

In this Garden setting, God not only spoke prophetically over the woman, but reminded Adam of his responsibility as head of his family. Not only are you to lead, cultivate, and speak life over her – but now you are going to have to provide for her. You, Adam, now have a new job description. I love the way the <u>Complete Jewish Bible</u> describes Genesis 3:17-19:

> To Adam he said, "Because you listened to what your wife said and ate from the tree about which I gave *you* the order, '*You are not to eat from it*,' the ground is cursed on your account; you will work hard to eat from it as long as you live. It will pro- duce thorns and thistles for you, and you will eat field plants. You will eat bread by the sweat of your forehead till you return to the ground – for you were taken out of it: you are dust, and you will return to dust."

First of all, Adonai addresses the issue of Adam's disobedience. Like a parent, He said, "I told **you** NOT to eat from it! But you totally dis-regarded My wishes and chose to listen to your wife, whom you allowed to be deceived. You heard Me, you heard the serpent, and you listened to your wife – then, you willingly chose to disobey. Your declaration of independence has now caused the very ground to be cursed! My provision for easily accessible food stops immediately. From now on, you will have to work hard to eat. Step up, Adam, you desired to be *like* Me, so now you will be the Provider for your family."

As harsh as this sounds, God – who is GOOD – is forcing Adam stand up and be the man he was intended to be! Adam was created to be courageous, truthful, responsible for his actions, and trustworthy in relationship. Everything and everybody around us is affected by our decisions in life. What we do and what we say has an effect on matters spiritually, physically, financially, mentally, and relationally.

In one day, because Adam disobeyed a command, allowed his wife to be deceived, deflected blame, was less than truthful, and was disrespectful to God (blaming Him for the woman)...the very ground was affected. Notice that God DID NOT curse man – but rather He cursed the ground. Interestingly, after this event the ground – which is living matter – has the ability to curse man! In Genesis 4:10-12 (NASB), after Cain [Kayin] murders Abel [Hevel], God says, *"The voice of your brother's blood is crying out to me from the ground! Now you are cursed from the ground, which has opened its mouth to receive your brother's blood at your hands. When you farm the ground it will no longer yield its strength to you. You will be a fugitive, wandering the earth."*

Man was not cursed on the day of "The Choosing", the ground was. Now Adam will have to spend the rest of his days doing what he learned to do in the Garden – cultivating and keeping the ground – but, to the "nth" degree. The ground, now cursed, will produce thorns and thistles. Work, intended for satisfaction and enjoyment, will be harder now.

Finally, because of Adam's brazenness when he blamed God for his actions, Father God reminds Adam of who he is. Adam, who may have secretly desired to be *like* God (if even for good intentions) is reminded that he "is dust". Ouch. Imagine hearing that from the God of this Universe! However, sometimes when we lack remorse, we need to be humbled.

Humility is the accurate assessment of one's worth in comparison to the deity they serve – it is truly knowing who we are.

God is God. He will always be God. Even in our most intimate, loving, Fatherly, husbandly times with Him – we are His creation, He is our Creator. He is telling Adam, "Every day that you work the ground, remember who you are, and that I am the One who created you."

Take a good look at the wilderness ground, Adam, for that is where you will return. I wonder if Adam thought, "Gulp. I'm a dead   man walking." For the very next thing he did was speak over his wife and declare her name to be "*Em*" [Eve] because she would be the "mother of all living[35]." Up until that point, she was "the woman", or *Ishshah* who was taken from Ish [man]. Adam, after having been loved *toughly* by Father God, stepped up to the plate and functioned in his purpose as head of the family unit – speaking life over the woman.

At the end of this encounter, Father God set about to provide covering for the couple as they would need it for their trip to their new home. I wonder if Adam and Eve watched while the Lord God chose which animals were to die on their behalf. These were creatures that lived peacefully with them in the Garden. Were they a close part of their family, like our pets with whom we become attached to? Whatever they were, I am sure God choose the perfect one(s) to clothe his beloved for the untamed environment of the wilderness.

Little did they know, eating from the forbidden tree did cause the people to become – in one essence - *like* the triune God, for now they knew good and evil. They would have to be banished from the Garden in order to keep them from eating from the Tree of Life and living forever. Humans, designed to live eternally, would now experience death. But the Sovereign God *knew* all of this before the foundations of the earth. He

---

[35] Genesis 3:20

would, one day, lay himself down and redeem (restore the value, buy back) mankind for Himself.[36]

As Adam and Eve walked away from the Garden, did Adam's strong arm hold up and console weeping Eve who was not from the wilderness?[37] Did they fear or feel abandoned because God did not walk with them, but drove man out? Did they understand that it was *they* who 'divorced' their Shepherd who leads with just the sound of His voice? Did they feel humiliated by being driven like cattle? Was there any remorse at this point? Did they have any understanding of how much their single act cost?

"It" cost mankind their life.

To save mankind, "it" cost our Savior *everything*.

---

[36] Revelation 5:9 (NASB) "For You were slain and did purchase for God with Your blood men from every tribe and tongue and people and nation."

[37] Although the Word says in Genesis 3:24, "So He [Lord God] drove the *man* out...", ultimately, Eve *chose* to go with the man. One can only ascertain whether they were driven out together or whether she followed later.

Heroes & Compasses
CHAPTER TEN

———————⌇———————

"...For the Lord has created a new thing in the land...

A female shall compass a man."

Jeremiah 31:22 – Amplified Bible

I can think of nothing worse than being banished. To know that everything you have come to know and love is still there, but you can never go back. This would be perpetual torment and scary as hell. Being removed is totally different than choosing to leave. Decisions are beds of our own choosing that we are then forced to lie in. But banishment bears the brunt of shame and disgrace.

There is nothing recorded about the days following Adam and Eve's expulsion from the Garden until we pick back up in the account of Cain (*Kayin*[38]) and Abel (*Hevel*[39]), their sons. From their sad story, one can glean a few pieces of information about the lives of Adam and Eve. In the time it took from leaving the Garden to at least the young manhood of their boys, we can assume the following:

▶ They were able to develop some kind of home and cultivate farmland;

---

[38] Kayin means "acquisition"
[39] Hevel mean "emptiness or vanity"

- ▶ Life was tough as evidenced by naming their second child Abel (*Hevel*); which means 'emptiness';

- ▶ They developed fortitude and 'survivability';

- ▶ They still had relationship with a God that loved them;

- ▶ They taught their children to reverence / worship the Lord with offerings;

- ▶ The family unit was dysfunctional – as evidenced by Cain's underlying anger.

I've heard it taught that first-borns look like their dad. In the secular college environment wherein it was delivered, the reasoning for this bio-logical similarity was that it helped the survival of the species because man would then bond with his look-alike offspring. When bonding occurs, the male will provide the nurturing and training needed for the family unit to thrive. *If* this statement is true – which, by the way, I have noticed that every true first-born I know does resemble the paternal side of the family – then we can assume that Cain looked, and very probably, acted like his dad.

Was Adam angry? Probably. One can only imagine how hard life had become for them. Not only did Adam have to clear the land on which to plant, but he had to manufacture the tools from raw materials to get the job done. In my mind, I see him laboring under the hot sun, struggling with a stubborn tree trunk, and digging around it for hours in an effort to drag it from its stronghold. Cain is nearby in the field, clearing it of rocks and watching his dad. He has learned to keep a safe distance from outbursts. Adam, nearly spent, pulls with all his might – but the trunk doesn't budge. With sweat dripping down his face and stinging his eyes, he is overtaken by the labyrinth of raw emotion and all he wants to do is cry. Even that makes him angry. Exasperated, he irreverently flings his fists at heaven and bellows at the top of his lungs. He can't form the words to this God he once walked with because it hurts too much, only a deep guttural sound escapes, "UGGHHH!!!" Staying at the far end of the field, Cain thinks to himself, *"It's going to be a rough night…"*

Outwardly, Adam would never admit it. But inwardly, he harbored resentment toward Eve, still blaming her for his predicament. Before her, life was easy. Sure, he was lonely, but he had a good thing going on. He didn't have someone whose mere presence reminded him of the failure he was. He was more than sick of her optimistic antidotes and empty encouragement, life sucked because of her. Then, on days like this, here he is in the sweltering heat while she sits in the shade churning milk/butter from one of Abel's goats. Lately, everything she did annoyed him. With that, he threw down his hand-twisted ropes and headed toward the house.

As she watched Adam march through the field in her direction, she was overcome with dread. Frantically, she quickly went through a list in her head of things that had to be done that day. Did she milk the animals, clean the house, mend the tattered clothes, and start the evening meal? Yes, yes and yes. Not knowing what he could possibly be mad at this time, she determined herself to be calm.

He came to a stop right in front of her and crossed his arms. Before she could say a word, he belted her with, "Did it even occur to you that I might have been thirsty working myself to death in this heat? No, probably not – seeing you're feeling quite fine just sitting in the shade! Is that what this marriage has come to – you only thinking about YOU??? I'm out there slaving away for the family, but you seem to always have time to sit. Must be nice!..."

After a long evening of hurtful words and hurt feelings, Adam and Eve, exhausted, lay down for the night. As each licked their respective wounds, they couldn't help but wonder, "How did we get *here*?" What was meant for perfection was now very dysfunctional. Angry Adam and Enabling Eve needed to find some way of working all this out.

God does not abandon us in these moments. One of the ways He honors mankind is by letting us figure our way out of messes (usually ones that we get ourselves into). Adam and Eve had, in days past, spent TIME in Love's Presence. They knew Love Himself. They just needed to figure out how to let Love compass the way.

Our GPS guidance system needs to be recalibrated from time to time. My husband and I encountered a difficult period while serving as new pastors for a church that endured a devastating split after the previous over-seers embezzled tens of thousands of dollars. Part of the congregation wanted us to be tarred and feathered, while the other part remained steadfast and faithful. It was a difficult period in life for us as we endured hurtful accusations and persecution. To add fuel to the fire, I was working four days a week, working on my master's degree full-time, and helping my husband in ministry the rest of the time.

The needs of the church and people in the community were taxing nearly all our resources. The emotional battle from those who wanted us out of there drained whatever was left of us, and little remained for the nurturing of our relationship. Over time, we started bickering and feeling resentful of one another. The navigational forces of difficulties were pulling us apart.

At the time, I worked for Northwood's Outfitters in Greenville, Maine, while finishing my master's degree. One winter afternoon, my boss, Mike Boutin, said, "Why don't you and Jesse take a couple of the snow machines and go for a ride … have some fun." Thinking it a great idea, Jesse began charting our course with the local guides who showed us the trail system and how to take a shortcut across the lake back to the shop when we were done. (Moosehead Lake, situated in the Longfellow Mountains, is approximately 40 miles long by 10 miles wide with a maxi-mum depth of 246 feet.)

It was a magnificent ride that afternoon through the mountains of the Maine Highlands Region; we couldn't have asked for better weather or conditions. What a lovely adventure! As the winter sun began to set, we headed for the trail that would bring us to the lake.

By the time we reached the lake, it was dark. We stopped for a moment and looked out across the expanse of wind-blown ice. I was a little nervous heading out on glare ice, but Jesse reassured me to just follow him across and shift my weight to the back of the machine.

As we started across in the dark, I had no clue that some deep spring under the lake had broken loose and was melting the ice from the bottom up. A few miles into the trip, Jesse started breaking through the ice ahead of me but could not stop on thin ice with a six-hundred-pound machine – he could only hope that I stayed behind him at full speed.

Unfortunately, his machine was weakening the already thin ice and my machine started to porpoise up and down. I tried to keep up with him and shifted my weight to the back of the sled to get better control. That's when I hit a clump of hard wind-blown snow, and it flipped my machine into the air. In slow motion, I landed on the ice and watched as the 600-pound machine landed on top of me. The crashing weight broke through the thin ice, pinning me under water. One of the skis and the back tow bar caught on some of the ice around the hole, suspending the machine on the hole over me.

I am not afraid of dying, but there was no way in hell that I wanted to die by drowning in a dark abyss under the expanse of ice! I grabbed hold of the precariously balanced upside-down machine, kicked with all my might, and reached frantically for solid ice. I finally managed to pull myself up on semi-solid surface. Then, lying flat-bellied I crawled apprehensively across the cracking weak ice until I was safely away from that awful hole.

Still breathing in panicked short gasps, I looked up to analyze my next action. That's when I spotted my husband's headlight far, far in the distance … disappearing into the black night. He had no idea that I had broken through – and even if he did, he couldn't stop because the ice had been cracking under him. I was alone, very alone. Despair welled up within me. What was I going to do? I prayed, *"Oh God … not like this. I don't want to die like this."* My words, like tiny puffs of smoke, hung visibly before me in the cold. Lying prostrate on the weak ice, I never felt more alone.

Then, I saw it! The little light far in the distance turned and headed in my direction. I was split inside. One part of me hollered into the darkness, "Go back! Go back! You'll break through! Go back!" The other part of me welcomed the hero heading back across the dangerous lake to get me.

Many men would not have done that. They *maybe*, once safe on the other shore, would call 911, then wait for those whose occupation requires risk to save me. Not my husband. Without a shadow of doubt, he would lay his life down for me.

I watched his headlight porpoise up and down across the dangerous lake, praying fervently for his safety. He stopped about fifty yards from me, and I scurried toward him first on my belly then running with arms wide open. Meeting me halfway, we embraced and wept together. He was overcome by almost losing me. I was overcome by the display of courageous love.

Then, this man of integrity said the most awful thing. He looked at the machine hanging upside-down precariously over the open hole in the ice and said, "We need to get that machine before it goes under."

"What??? No, Honey. I don't want to go anywhere near that hole!"

"We have to. It's not our machine." he replied.

Sighing, I relented. We worked our way over to the hole and with him on one side and me on the other; we carefully flipped the sputtering machine over. Ice cracked all around us. Quickly my husband directed the work. We would both grab hold of the back tow bar and pull the heavy machine toward thicker ice – all the while depending on the skis to hold tight to the grip they had on the hole's edge. When the weight of the sled shifted, we would break through and tread water. Still holding the back bar, we would work our way to thicker ice and do it again.

We tediously worked the heavy machine onto more stable ice – inch by inch. When it finally sat on a layer of soft ice which sunk under the weight, Jesse instructed me to work the throttle and run next to it but get it out of there! Trusting his judgment, I did as he said and worked the machine over near his parked sled and waited.

When he made his way over, we stood wet and cold and looked at one another. I waited for his next instruction – all I wanted was off that lake!

He said, "We are going to head back to the trailhead where we came on. This time I am going to follow you."

I gulped. Although I didn't want to be left alone again, I panicked because this girl was born without a GPS system. I have no navigational skills. I get lost in the grocery store.

He pointed a direction and off we went. Tears ran out of the bottom of my helmet as I prayed with all my heart, *"Lord, help me. I have no idea where to go!"*

Suddenly, out of the heavens, a meteor appeared. It sped through the sky and exploded in a direction ahead of us, lighting up the night sky. I headed in that direction – scared, cold, hurt, and crying. *"Lord, get me off this lake. Please, Lord, I want off this lake!"*

I kept heading in the direction of where the meteor exploded – working hard to keep from losing control of the machine again on the slick ice. Before long, I spotted the exact trailhead where we first entered the lake!

When I reached the firm snow-covered land, I stopped the machine, jumped off and ran into my husband's arms. I sobbed in his embrace. It was then that I told him that I was hurt.

We made our way home (the long way, avoiding any lake travel) to shed our wet winter clothing. Once there, Jesse saw my leg – black from the bruising of a 600-pound machine landing on top of me. He immediately took me to the hospital to rule out any blood clots.

All ended well with this real-life adventure. Not only did God show up in all His glory and guide us safely off that lake, but my husband (without a doubt) laid down his life for me that day when he came back for me.

Just as God told the young prophet, Jeremiah[40], I was serving as my husband's compass by changing his direction. Jesse would later tell me that there was never a question in his mind about him turning around and res- cuing me – that's what heroes do.

I am quite certain that had my husband not turned around and saved me - whether I lived or died - he would have beat himself up for the rest of his life. He needed to do that for him as much as it was for me. We were created in the image of God to be heroes, not cowards. We are over-comers who can lay "it" down for others because His love in us compels us to do so!

In this adventure called "Life", our lives play out the gospel story. In everyday events, "it" matters to God, "it" matters to others, and "it" even matters to yourself to know that when the chips are down, you can be depended upon!

---

[40] Jeremiah 31:22 – "…a female shall compass a man." Scripture taken from THE AMPLI-
FIED BIBLE, Old Testament copyright © 1965, 1987 by the Zondervan Corporation.
Used by Permission.

Life Happens
CHAPTER ELEVEN

———————⌒———————

"...and the tongue is a fire, the very world of iniquity,

The tongue is set among our members as that which

defiles the entire body,

and sets on fire the course of our life..."

James 3:6 (NASB)

Along the way relationships get broken, we let people down, storms (physical and spiritual) come, finances fail, and houses fall. Life happens.

What happens when we can't fix everything? What happens when we feel like we've totally blown "Plan A" for our life and we're barely keeping our head above water in "Plan B"? Do we walk around resentful, blaming God and everyone else for our problems? Do we become bitter human beings, spreading our poison everywhere we go? Many do.

The truth is, we are usually where we're at because we've been *speaking* it. Life oftentimes comes to us exactly how we've ordered it. Out of the abundance of our heart...our mouths speak.[41] Simply put; we act upon what we think about. Adultery doesn't just 'happen', rather we act out

---

[41] Matthew 12:34

what we've thought. Oftentimes, we are spiritually oppressed because we, with our mouth, gave permission for the enemy to have authority over us in areas! I've heard it said that life is only 10% of what happens to us and 90% our reaction to it.

We need to change the way we think because our "selves" will go where we see our "selves". For example, I struggled with my weight all through my adolescent years. I didn't eat large portions, and I was very active, but my body just hung on to extra weight. Then, one day when I was getting ready for work, I heard the Holy Spirit ask me, "What are you thinking about?"

Looking in the mirror, I thought for a moment and answered, "What I am going to fix for a quick breakfast." Then I continued with my morning routine.

About 10:00 a.m. while at my desk at work, I heard Him asking again, "What are you thinking about?"

Catching my thought, I replied, "Where I am going for lunch today." Then, I continued with work.

While working through a pile of paperwork about 3:00 p.m., I heard His voice again, "What are you thinking about?"

I quickly responded with, "What I am going to make for dinner tonight." Then, I continued proofing the documents before me.

After dinner and a walk, as I sat reading a book, I heard His voice yet again, "What are you thinking about?"

Even though my mind was reading the pages before me, my thoughts were mentally searching the kitchen cupboards wondering what I was going to fix for a little snack. It was then that the Holy Spirit brought conviction upon me. All day long my thoughts were consumed with food and eating. This sickened me.

Right there in my living room, I fell to my knees and repented. Rather than my thought-life being focused on the One I professed to love and serve, it remained fixated on the self-gratification of eating. I cried out to God for forgiveness and asked Him to change the way I think. *"Please Lord, give me YOUR thoughts! Change my mind – that it may be set upon YOU!"*

My mind didn't change overnight. But, slowly, over time I noticed that there were days that I missed meals because I simply forgot to eat! Then, because my mind was set on Him more often, I began to feel His heart on matters and felt compelled to fast on a more regular basis. Thirty- seven years later, I am 50 pounds lighter than I was at twenty!

As obesity rates began to climb in the late 90's, causing even the fashion industry to alter their sizing and marketing, it concerned me especially with those professing to be "ultra-spiritual-Christians". Judgmentally, I found it hard to trust the integrity of ministers and teachers if they, in my eyes, lacked discipline. Trying to shake my judgmental attitude and take on the mind of Christ, I asked Jesus one day how He felt about His people getting so fat.

As I stood on the stage that day, looking out over the largely overweight crowd at our church in Tallahassee, Florida, my heart broke. I saw Jesus walking by each one of them, and as He did, He allowed me to hear their thoughts.

"I am so fat."

"I hate the way I look."

"She's so thin – I hate her."

"I'm hungry. I wish he'd shut up so we can go eat."

"These pants are strangling me."

He looked at me with tears streaming down His face, and said, "They don't even notice Me and I am right in front of them."

I cried with Him that day, not only for the people, but because my judgmental heart was broken. The issue wasn't what they weighed, but what they thought. What a privilege to have His thoughts become my thoughts! I declared that day, "Lord, help me from here on out to see through Your eyes and hear through Your ears!"

Oh, that we would change the way we think! In Luke 21:14-19, Jesus says [paraphrased]:

> *So make up your minds beforehand not to justify yourselves, but when " life happens" and things get tough, be in such relationship with ME that because you are thinking with MY thoughts, My words of wisdom will pour right out of your mouth!*

Jesus doesn't change people's lives by badgering or condemning them. Rather, He LOVES them right on into relationship with Him! Through this process, He uses us - as vessels – to lavish His love upon His people, speaking His love language to them!

Jesus prompts us to make up our *minds* – adjust our thoughts – and choose beforehand to allow His love to flow through us. In the context of the Luke's passage, He says, it will even be those closest to us – parents, brothers, relatives, and friends – that will cause us grief and even deliver us over to death.

When reading this, our spiritually-righteous selves, tend to think, *"In the last days, if I am turned over by anyone for the cause of Christ...I will go to my death for Him!"* But, what if – in these last days – your friend, sister, brother, or Pastor offends you? I have seen many "super-spiritual" people gather together their little band of supporters and storm out of a Church Body and seek its destruction for the rest of their days. Likewise, what if your family or parents hurt you? Counseling rooms are filled with bitter 'victims' who live their days blaming someone else for their woes, and prayer altars are frequented regularly by those who hang on to their wounds, choosing to believe the lies of those whose opinions they think matter.

All these woes can be avoided if we determine *beforehand* to LOVE. We've already been warned that they *will* turn on us, they *will* offend us, they *will* let us down, and they *will* hurt us. It should come as no surprise when "it" happens.

"It" happened to me one day in 1992. My divorce had been finalized and after I had been living in a camper with our youngest son, my long-time good friend, Sharon, offered her house in Jacksonville, Florida for us to start all over again. I had already sent my meager belongings up to her place and was finishing up my last day at work in south Florida. However, after saying good-byes to my co-workers and walking out the door that led to a new life, I was greeted by a Sheriff Deputy that served me with a court order. It stated that I was deemed to be a danger to myself and my child and that I could not travel outside of the county boundaries until further court hearings. (I learned from my ex-husband that one can file *anything* against another without due cause – I was even brought before the court as an 'unfit mother' because I made my children attend church with me!)

I was devastated. What was I to do now? ALL my belongings, even my blow-dryer, were in Jacksonville, Florida. I had nowhere to live, and now, after saying good-bye to my boss and co-workers … no job.

I needed income – so I turned abruptly and went back inside the workplace and asked for my job back. They gladly gave it. But where would we live? I immediately thought about the safety of my grandparents' home and that welcome dining table in the kitchen. So, I drove out to their house and asked if Matthew and I could live on their "Florida Room/Porch" (a closed-in porch) until I could get a court hearing. They said yes.

Ten-year-old Matthew and I moved into their porch area with our suitcases. Within a week or so, I became alarmed when I smelled something burning. I called an electrician who confirmed that the wiring in the entire wall was sparking and melting together. I paid for him to re-wire an entire wall in their house. Then, when their dishwasher quit working, I bought them a new one and had it installed. As the days passed, I bought groceries, washed their car, and kept the place clean in gratitude for their hospitality. My ex-husband's lawyer – best in her field – kept the case out of court for months on end.

As "life" would happen, Grandma was diagnosed with colon cancer and scheduled for surgery. My aunt, who lived in Alaska, decided to come down and help her mother recuperate. It was only days before Matthew and I started overhearing snide remarks from her concerning us. She overlooked all that I was doing for my grandparents in return for their letting me stay there; and before long, we couldn't even walk across the floor 'right'. In an effort to stay out of her way, we spent more time at work, the church, and ate meals away from the family.

Then, one Wednesday night after church, Matthew and I walked into an 'intervention' circle consisting of my grandma, grandpa, mom, and aunt. I was asked to sit down. After weeks of being badgered by my aunt and hearing over and over again that I was a "free-loader" who needed to get out, my grandma abruptly informed me that I needed to move.

Gutted, I asked, "When do I have to move?" Grandma answered, "By Monday."

Defying court order and holding back tears, I packed up my and Matthew's few belongings and headed to my brother's house in Tallahassee, Florida. I had to get away.

We spent Thursday through Sunday far away from all the mess and just enjoyed my brother's company. On Sunday evening, as we made the long drive back to south Florida, Matthew looked at me and said, "Mama, do we still have to move?"

I glanced at him and said, "Yes, Honey. It looks like we do."

"Where are we moving?" he asked

"I don't know, Honey. I don't know. But let's pray about it."

There in that car, we held hands and prayed a simple prayer, "Father, you clothe the lilies of the field, and You see when the sparrow falls from the tree. We are your children, and we need a place to live." I was too choked up to pray anything more.

We arrived back at my grandparents' house well after dark. As I unloaded the car, something just didn't seem right. I finally walked into the living room and asked Grandma, "Where is Aunt Arlie?"

Grandma replied, "Ohhh...you wouldn't believe it. Just shortly after you left, she walked into the kitchen to get a drink and slipped on something. She's in the hospital with a broken hip." Hmmmm...I couldn't help but wonder...*which angel PUSHED her down???* ☺

Some folks would be so hurt by their family right now, that nothing would prevent them from walking out and never come back. In their pride, they would justify, *"Fine...if they don't want me – I don't want them! They'll miss me when I'm gone, though."* But I had determined *beforehand* to love a family who did not know God. So, I sat down with Grandma and offered, "Aunt Arlie came down here to help you after your surgery. It's obvious that she won't be able to do that now. If you want, I will stay on and take care of both of you."

Not knowing what else to do, my grandma replied, "Well... I guess you'll have to."

Throughout the following weeks, I cooked, cleaned, and tended to my grandparents and sour aunt. Day after day, I would reach through the calloused wall surrounding my aunt and touch her. I went out of my way to make her comfortable. When she criticized my cooking, I would bite my lip and tell her I would try harder next time. After a couple weeks, I knew she needed to exercise a bit and get some fresh air. So, I prepared a sitting place for her and Grandma out on the patio and helped them both out there. After a short while, I showed up with a tub of water and a razor. I sat next to Aunt Arlie and gently placed her leg in my lap. She was flabbergasted and demanded to know what I was doing. Without saying a word, I lovingly applied the gel to her leg and tenderly began shaving it. Defiantly, she crossed her arms across her chest and sat rigidly. As I stroked her leg,

I talked softly and kindly to her – telling her how much I appreciated her coming down to help. By the time I finished shaving her legs, her arms lay softly across her midriff, and she actually smiled.

I ended up outlasting (and out-loving) my aunt. When she was well enough, we put her on a plane back to Alaska. Paradoxically, my feelings lined up with my resolve (my mindset and thoughts) and I really did fall in love with her.

Then, as a reward of my decision to love instead of harbor bitterness, I had the wonderful privilege of being with Grandma through her final days. The cancer had spread to her brain, and she would waver between this world and the next. There were times she was mentally *with* me and as I changed her adult diaper, she would weep and apologize. I would pat her on the hinny and tell her, "Grandma, I would plant a big kiss on this buttock if you didn't stink so bad!" Then, we would laugh.

Then, she would have days when she drifted into another realm where we would lie together on the bed and make imaginary pancakes and talk about issues that were *real* in her head. One day, near the end, she started talking to people that weren't there. I recognized the names of these people as ones who had already passed on. So, I asked her what they were saying. She said, "They want me to cross the river."

I said, "Do you want to cross?" She replied, "Oh, yes!"

"Then, go on across, Grandma." Sadly, she said, "I can't."

"Why?"

"Because I can't swim", she replied.

I said, "Grandma, I have a feeling that if you trust God and start across that river, He'll get you across."

It wasn't long after that, that she passed, and I had the honor of officiating her funeral. I can't wait to see her again. I just kind of think that she already has a pot of coffee brewing for our next long visit...

We have choices when 'life happens' and "it" matters to God how we choose. I don't have it in me to love the un-lovable – in fact, I don't even like them. But I do have it in me to set *my* feelings aside and let God love them *through* me. He will love them right into His arms if we allow "it". Is "it" easy? Emphatically, no! Is "it" worth it? Definitely, YES!"

Willing & Adaptable
CHAPTER TWELVE

———————⌒———————

"...God is opposed to the proud, but gives

Grace to the humble...

Submit therefore to God..."

James 4:6-7 (NASB)

An amazing thing happens when we choose beforehand to be *willing* and *adaptable* with God and with others. Religious folk (those who kindly apply the Law to others) would call this act…"submit". This word, not used in its proper context, immediately provokes an inward rebuttal. Telling someone to 'submit' is like rubbing sandpaper on their soul. Even little children resist the command to 'submit'. That's because its implication is contrary to God's heart.

Over the centuries, man has errantly translated the love-language word: *hupotassó*. This word, used correctly, describes our *willingness* to place ourselves under Christ's direction, responsibility, and rule. It implies that we adapt, yield, permit, defer to, and surrender to what He wants (His will). As we *hupotassó* (submit) to Christ, we trust Him enough that we choose to become 'willingly adaptable.' When we do this, it is not out of obedience to a harsh command, but rather, an act of love. It is us responding to His LOVE toward us.

In James 4:6, it says, "...God is opposed to the proud, but gives grace to the humble." The first part of this verse states God's position regarding the "proud". The Greek word, *huperĕphanos*, refers to one that is "over" or one who shows himself above his fellow men in honor preferring himself[42]. God stands in direct contradiction to those who lift their chins and attempt to control others through whatever justification they have rationalized.

On the contrary, a humble (*tapeinos*) man accurately assesses who he is in comparison to the deity he serves. We are the creation, He is the Creator. That will never change. Because this is so, James continues with, "*hupotassó* (submit) therefore to God." Our response to Love, is to place our self under Love. He also continues in James 4:10 (paraphrased): "When you recognize who you are in His presence, He will exalt you."

Putting this in practice in our response to others is not easy. It is one thing to be willing & adaptable (*hupotassó*) to a perfect and loving God, but it is entirely a different matter concerning all the imperfect people in our lives. The difficulty is compounded even more so when we are in day-to-day relations with those closest to us. Yet, Paul exhorts us in Ephesians 5:21 to "submit one to another in reverence of Christ."

Maybe it's a good thing Paul never married. In counseling, I find it easy to stand on the outside of a glass house and render familial advice to others. Even researching and writing this book has been easier than trying to apply the truths to my own marriage. Over the years, though, God has given me bits and pieces of a grand puzzle. Some were nuggets of truth dropped into my spirit, others were heart-wrenching experiences where truth was learned through practical application.

One of the most abused truths in marital relationships is that of "submitting". Paul refers to this in his response to the Corinthians, wherein

---

[42] Hebrew-Greek Key Word Study Bible, New American Standard Bible: AMG Publishers, Chattanooga, TN, 1990.

some of the new believers were having problems in their marriages. Counseling them in I Corinthians chapter 7, Paul reminds them in verse 23, *"You were bought with a price; do not become slaves of men."* Our spouse does not own us. We are God's children - different, yet equal.

I remember a day shortly after my first tumultuous marriage that I lay weeping before the Lord. Earlier that evening, I had asked a Godly woman, whom I highly respected, to be my mentor through wellness. She pondered for a moment then replied, "No." I was heart-broken. When I asked "why", she responded with, "Because you think you are a victim."

"But I AM a victim!"

"No, you're not." she replied.

"But I didn't ask to be physically and mentally treated that way!" She calmly stated, "You are not a victim."

I left the house emotionally gutted. As I lay there that night, I knew I needed inner-healing, and I begged God to apply His balm over my heart to heal all the wounds inflicted by *that* man. I recited a list of offenses that occurred throughout the twelve years together. Before the Judge of the Universe, I self-righteously declared my ex-husband to be a wretched horrible monster. After hearing enough of my case, the Holy Spirit (who is the One who *"elegchō"* – convicts by exposing truth and revealing reality from God's perspective), spoke into my spirit saying, *"Rather than a victim, you have become the 'chiefest' of sinners. You dethroned God in your life and replaced Him with man. You became a people-pleaser. Instead of pleasing God, you wasted all your time and energy trying to please and be affirmed by man. You are an IDOLATOR."*

Gulp. What could I say? It was true. I, who had been bought with a great price, became a slave to man. I craved man's affirmation. Ultimately, though, I served a cruel god. The more I was mistreated, the more I tried to please.

In a healthy marriage, there is supposed to be a triune desire to please. Paul, looking in from the outside of a glass house, refers to it as 'divided interests'.[43] We are, first and foremost, to devote ourselves to pleasing the Lord. Then, out of our devotion to God, we seek ways to please our wife or husband.

At the beginning of I Corinthians 7, Paul starts out with "...*it is good for a man not to touch a woman.*" The Greek word for 'touch' is "*haptomai*" which means to touch with an ulterior motive to get what he wants or with the intent to manipulate. The same can be said of a woman.

Then, in verse 3 of this same chapter, he says, "*Let the husband fulfill his duty to his wife, and likewise also the wife to her husband.*" The Greek word for 'duty' (*eunola*) means good will or benevolence. Every day we should ask God how we can bless our spouse and minister kindness to them. This is important to God. He loves to be personally involved in relationships that portray His love to the world!

In the middle of this passage about marriage, Paul acknowledges that sometimes relationships get out of balance – either one spouse is a believer and the other is not, or one spouse is dominating the other. Although it was common in that culture to have arranged marriages or even slaves, I personally think Paul [in the context of marriage] was writing to those whose marriages were not ideal. After years of pastoral counseling, Jesse and I have found there are many marriages where one partner is not fulfilling their duty [*eunola*: good will, benevolence] to their spouse. In many, where both spouses are working, the husband comes home and basically does what he wants. Meanwhile, the wife by nature of default; makes dinner, starts the laundry, cleans the kitchen, bathes the kids, takes out the garbage, feeds the animals, makes lunches for the next day, folds loads of clothes – then looks at her snoring husband with a sigh (in some cases the roles are reversed and the man carries the domestic load).

---

[43]   I Corinthians 7: 32-34

Is performing a kind act of love going to be an easy task? Far from it! In verse 28 of I Corinthians 7 Paul writes, "But if you should marry… [you] will have *trouble*[44] in this life and I am trying to spare you." Marriage is hard – real hard. We're not always very loveable. Life happens, hormones happen (God and I are going to have a long talk about hormones one day), feelings get hurt, miscommunication occurs, wedges are driven, careers take turns, it takes energy to raise children, birthdays and anniversaries are forgotten, and we neglect to romance one another. ONLY by us seeking God first will we have the initiative to fulfill our responsibility of treating our spouse with undeserved kindness. Love does indeed cover a multitude of sins.

There was a cold winter day when it seemed all these maladies occurred. Life was tough while my second husband, Jesse, recovered after a drunk driver hit him. We ended up living in a 15' x 34' cabin in the 'bush' outside of Talkeetna, Alaska. We had no electricity or running water and took showers at a truck stop when we couldn't stand the smell of one another any longer. As the seasonal darkness set in one evening, Jesse and I started arguing about something that was so very unimportant. But through the unfolding of raw emotions and tough times, hurtful words were hurled through the tense atmosphere. My husband was an intimidating foe. He towered over me with strength of volume and words to defeat any enemy. I retreated, long-underwear clad, to our bed and pulled the covers over my head and wept.

In my mind, Jesse relished over the victory and waited before coming bed – just to show that he had no intention of apologizing for his rash words over me. When he finally crawled in bed, I made sure I was as far on the side as I could be. Silent tears slid off the side of the bed as I made my case to Abba. I recalled every hurtful word and unkind look hurled my way through the night…and cried big crocodile tears that made a little puddle on floor.

---

[44] Some versions state, "tribulation".

Then, the Holy Spirit spoke. He said, *"Reach over and touch your husband."*

"What??? Really? You want ME to touch HIM? Did you not hear what he said to me?"

Silence.

After a moment, He spoke again, *"Reach over and touch your husband."*

Now the tears really flowed. How could a just God – a God who loved me – ask me to do such a thing? Unfair! Totally unfair!

For the third time, the Holy Spirit said, *"Reach over and touch your husband."*

It is one thing to ignore God when He says something once – but to disregard what He wants three times ... I knew I had better comply; if only out of obedience [He does own the elements and can direct lightning wherever He chooses]. Sigh.

"So ... fine. He wants me to touch my husband, does He? Well then..."

Still hanging off the side of the bed, I slowly stretched my leg across the wide chasm between us and touched my husband's leg with my big toe ... and he melted. The rigidness of his body softened, and Peace once again enveloped our marriage bed.

Looking back, I don't even remember what we argued about or exactly what hurtful words were hurled through the battleground. But I do remember the triune involvement in our relationship because I chose to let go of the offense and submit (be willing and adaptable) to the voice of God.

I agree with Paul who, in counseling the Corinthians, said [paraphrased], "In marriage, there will be trouble." The very term, marriage, is a black-smith's term. To marry two pieces together, requires intense heat, pounding iron against iron, more heat and more pressure – until the two pieces become one. A good blacksmith will marry two pieces of metal together so well that you cannot tell where one begins and the other ends – they are one.

Paul concludes chapter seven of his first letter to the Corinthians by admitting that a husband and wife may become distracted and momentarily lose that connection with God because their focus should be on how they may please one another.[45] Although Paul, a single man, saw that as a bad thing; I, on the other hand, think that defines healthy relationship.

What if we woke up every morning and asked God, "How would you like for me to bless my spouse today?"

What would life look like if we waited in expectation for any little moment in our day that we could do something to please God by blessing our partner in life?

I learned a valuable lesson about submitting from a young couple, John and Taffy, who came into our life not long after I reached my toe across the chasm and touched Jesse day. To set the backdrop, leading up to this red-letter day, one needs to understand what Jesse and I had been through and how God was using devastating events to break through our self-serving pride.

In the winter of 1999, as much as I would like to toot my own horn, I now admit that I harbored resentment and anger after that troubled man – a very drug-induced and drunk man - almost killed my husband. In an instant we were flung into a five-year nightmare. Jesse's injuries included: five ruptured disks in his back, three ribs separated from his spine, a broken collarbone and shoulder, a devastating frontal lobe [brain] injury, and his vision was reduced to 2% monocular [later he battled with blindness and wondered whether he would lose his vision permanently]. Because we were not in good hands with a certain insurance company, we had to sell everything for pennies-on-the-dollar just to keep him in therapy. The only thing we could afford after that was a little cabin in the wilderness of Alaska.

---

[45] I Corinthians 7:32-35

Since Jesse had therapy five days a week, there was no way he could work for another company – and in his mind, one does not ask the public for assistance if one is able to be productive in some way. So, we bought a used table saw and Stubblefield Construction was birthed. Prior to the accident, I was a corporate director of five successful companies. After the accident, I read every *Fine Homebuilding* magazine I could get my hands on in an effort to learn the construction trade. I knew it was important that he *work through* this storm we were in.

It was tough watching my husband, who once had an IQ of over 170 in math, struggle with finding the answer to two-plus-two in his head. He had to find new neural pathways in his brain to accomplish the simplest tasks in life. On the job, I would get things set up and do what I knew to do until old synapses were found in his head and he would then oversee the work. He was (and is) a very skilled craftsman and I was amazed and very proud of the beautiful work his hands made.

Day after day, we would make the long drive in from the bush in Talkeetna to the jobs in Wasilla and Anchorage. We would work until the doctor's appointment for that day, spend hours in therapy, then work till late each night – only to drive hours back on icy roads to the little cabin in the woods. Every now and then, God would show up and provide a breath-taking late-night show of His Aurora Borealis.

After nearly a year of this and virtually no advertising (all word-of-mouth referrals), our little construction company grew, and we were able to hire a crew. Even more thrilling was the potential to move closer to our jobs. Perusing through the classifieds, we thought we found an affordable house to rent in Wasilla, so Jesse called the Real Estate agent. However, he happened to dial the wrong phone number. On the other end there was another valley Real Estate agent who, after meeting us, said she happened to have something that we may want to look at. She knew of a family who was looking for the right people to take care of their beautiful home for a few years. In return for caretaking, our monthly rent was very affordable.

Long story short, we ended up living at the end of Endeavor Street (so apropos!) in a beautiful home on a 40-acre lakefront tract, with a heated airplane hangar, large garage, and three bathrooms! After we moved into the home and not dependent on an outhouse - sometimes I would walk by a bathroom and flush the toilet – just because I could!

It was at this time that we needed to focus a bit more on advertising our company and figured we needed a nice sign. My husband had a design in his head of a white buffalo along with the company name and things we specialized in. However, the size and design of this sign was more than we could afford at the time. One day, driving through Wasilla, Jesse happened to notice a new sign company and he pulled in. This young couple, John and Taffy, were working on their new shop and living quarters. Striking up a conversation with them, Jesse learned that they were having trouble designing a custom staircase – one of my husband's specialties – and a deal was worked out.

Soon after, we showed up to work in their home/workshop on this custom job. Tediously, we worked together on every rung, spindle, and handrail piece. One evening as Taffy and I were on the upper level painting the intricate spindles, her husband, John, hollered up from the first floor and asked, "Taff, can you come help me for a minute down here?" Her immediate response was, "I would love to." She sat her paintbrush aside and bounded down the unfinished staircase to him.

I was stunned by her immediate willingness to respond to his request for her assistance. Up to that point in my relationship with my husband, I justified that if I was there helping him, he should be happy with that. If he requested an extra hand with something and I was busy, I would respond, "I'll be there in a moment as soon as I finish with (fill in the blank)."

Furthermore, I extended this mindset into my relationship with the Lord. Often, when I felt the Lord's prompting, I would rationalize, "Lord, I know you want me to call so-and-so, but they will require too much time right now, so I will call them later. Or, Lord, I am busy doing (this or that) right now, I will spend time with you after I am done."

I peeked through the spindles and watched the loving relationship of John and Taffy as she helped him work through a difficult area of the staircase and asked the Holy Spirit to help me respond to my husband's requests for me with a more loving attitude. I knew if I could practice day-after-day love responses to my husband, it would affect my relationship with my Lord. Being willing and adaptable with our mate is in direct correlation to our relationship with God. Submission is important - *"It"* matters to us, to others, and to God.

Love is a Choice
CHAPTER THIRTEEN

———◇———

"A new commandment I give to you,

that you love one another,

even as I have loved you, that you also

love one another.

By this all men will know that you are My disciples,

if you have love for one another."

John 13:34-35 (NASB)

I'll never forget the day – September 11, 2001 – as I, and most of America, sat glued to television screens and watched in horror as terrorists carried out their gruesome attacks on innocent people. There was a sense of helplessness as plane after plane slammed into the World Trade Center and The Pentagon. As the unprecedented scenario unfolded, we eventually applauded the sacrificial heroes of Flight 93 that gave their lives to divert another attack to a populated area.

I mourned that day. I mourned for the loss of life, loss of national security, and for a son who served in the United States Army. He no longer served in an era of peace but now would taste the ugliness of war.

Prior to his departure to the Middle East with orders in hand, my husband and I had the privilege of spending time with his troop of young men. Jesse spent the last precious moments with our son and his friends going over every survival skill and combat tactic he could think of. I, on the other hand, spoke divine provision over them, supernatural protection, and every practical advice a mama could think of like; wash your feet, keep the Word near your heart (a metal-cased Bible given as a gift – it may save your life!), and turn your underwear inside-out to extend the time between changes. It seems a little silly now, but at the time, it was important that our son know all these things.

All of us aged during that deployment into battle. And, although those young men returned safely, none of us were ever quite the same after that. Innocence was lost. Friends were lost. There was nothing this mom and dad could do to make things better and soothe the war-tattered souls. We could only stand back and let God be God in their lives.

I am sure Jesus felt the same trepidation leading into the Last Supper. Knowing what lay ahead, this was His last time to impart whatever wisdom He could into those that would soon encounter life's greatest test.

In the various Gospel accounts of this event, Yeshua:

▶ Showed them what leadership looked like as He washed the feet of His disciples;

▶ Foretold of His betrayal;

▶ Broke up an argument about who was going to be the greatest in the Kingdom;

▶ Tells them that He is going to prepare a place for His Bride and will return for her;

▶ He teaches them more about relationship and His desire that they live in unity with one another as He does with His Father;

▶ Promises to send the Spirit of Truth, the "*Paracletos*" whose name literally means "come hither" – to help, lead, and guide us;

▶ Leaves His beloved with a new commandment to love one another.

This new commandment to love was a little baffling to me. He didn't remind them to love, but rather, mandated that they love one another. Was I missing something? Wouldn't it seem *natural* to love others, especially after hanging out with Jesus day-after-day? Loving should be an expected extension of abiding in Him (John 15:10).

After issuing this directive to love, He tells them that everyone will know they are true disciples if they have love for one another. Period. This, however, contradicts what we have heard from highly respectable people in our life. From wee lads we were told that good Christians, *must* not drink, smoke, or cuss. We also need to go to church (ugh! We don't go *to* church ... we *are* the church!). Furthermore, we need to learn how to speak 'Christianeze' (you know... sanctification, justification, consecration, propitiation, et al). Along the way, we also became accustomed to judging one's spirituality by how much they give, what they look like, or what position they hold – all man's criteria for spiritual-rightness.

God's criteria is complexingly simple. (Complexingly is a new word I made up – but it makes sense here.) If it were easy, there would be no need to command us to do it. Yet ... if we want right relationship with God – we just simply need to love others. How hard can that be? Evidently pretty dang hard when we are dealing with the unlovable, the broken part of humanity, the hurting people going around hurting people.

Jesus continued pouring His heart out at that supper. In chapter 15 of John, He revisits this commandment to love. He tells them:

> *This is My commandment, that you love one another, just as I have loved you. Greater love has no one than this, that one lay down his life for his friends. You are My friends, if you do what I command you. John 15:12-14 (NASB)*

Along the way, translating His words from one language to another, the passage has lost some meaning. When He mandates that we "love one another", the word He used for "love" is "*Agapaō*" which means "a direction of the will". He is telling us that love is a choice. We choose to love someone whether we *feel* like it or not, even if they haven't earned it.

As an example, He says that we do this by laying down our life for others. Yes, my Savior laid down His life for me – that I understand, and without thought, I would even jump in front of a bullet or speeding train for my family. But how does one lay down their life in the everyday scope of living?

The second type of love, the "greater love", that He refers to is the word "*Agapé*" which is "benevolent love, the giving of what is needed - not necessarily what is wanted." This is God-love. In John 3:16 He says, "God so *loved* (*agape*) the world that He gave..." God so loved us that He gave us what we needed – not necessarily, what man wanted.

If the Creator of the Universe were to show up in your room today (as He did with Solomon) and ask you what you wanted, many of us would probably choose: an easy life, wisdom, wealth, beauty, favor, justice, or power. Isn't that what people want?

Instead, the Father, who loves us so much, gave His only begotten Son – because it was *Salvation* that we needed. I don't think we quite understand the enormity of this gift. Many of us have only been taught that we need to escape (be saved from) eternal death. But Jonah 2:9 says, "Salvation is from the Lord." The Hebrew word for "Salvation" is "*Yshûwâh*". Yeshua [Jesus] IS Salvation! Better yet ... the root of this word is "*Yâsha*", which means "wide, open, and free"! When we receive Yeshua as Lord and Savior, not only are we going to live forever with Him, but because we receive Him personally to live inside of us, He enables us to live wide, open, and free!!!

Isn't that a better gift than what we thought we wanted from God? As a good parent, He gave us everything we needed. That is *agape* love – the "greater love" in John 15:13.[46]

This kind of love causes a person to lay down their *life* for others. The Greek word here for "life" is *"psuché"*, which refers to a person's soul or self. Yeshua's commandment was for us to *"agapaō"* or choose to love whether we felt like it or not – and to give of our "self". What does that look like?

Our "self" is the inner "me" that wants to do what it wants to do when it wants to do it. It's the question I pose whenever asked to volunteer or give of my time, "What's in it for me?" It's difficult to love someone with this sacrificial kind of love, because there is nothing in it for *me*. My struggle is more intense when the other person doesn't deserve this kind of time and attention from me. I struggle even more because I receive nothing in return; no atta-girl, no fan club, and no crowns dropping from heaven. Instead, I often feel like another piece of "me" just died.

In fact, there are times in my life that I have nothing left to give. It seems that the people around me are blood-thirsty "takers" that suck every ounce of life out of me. When it's ME that needs a hug, it's the very time I am required to give a hug. When it's ME that has had a hard day and could really use a foot massage, that's the time when I pull out the oil and towel and give my weary husband a foot-rub.

If there is one important thing I have learned in ministry, it is … you cannot give out of your need, it must come out of your over-flow. How then, can we lay down our life for others and love with this agape God-type love? Simply put … we can't.

One day, as I meditated on *Salvation* living *in* me – Yeshua living *in* me – it dawned on me that I John 4:16 says, "God is Love [*agape*]…" Wow! *Agapé* lives **in** me. I am like a walking tea-pot full of *agapé*. I don't need to muster up the will to love someone with what is needed at the time – I just need to dispense HIM. (Like I said earlier, complexingly *simple*.)

---

[46] "Greater love has no one than this, that one lay down his life for his friends." (NASB)

If someone needs a hug, I walk over, wrap my arms around them, and pour out Love (God). If kind words are needed in a moment, I open my mouth and let Love pour out. If a person needs comfort, I just sit next to them in silence and **let Love be Love**. So easy!

The BEST part is that I am not a spiritual guru gathering a little fan club that thinks I'm their savior. I am only the conduit that LOVES people into relationship with Yeshua – because it is HIM I am dispensing, not me.

You see, "it" really is that complexingly simple – if we choose it to be.

The Gift of Out-Loving
CHAPTER FOURTEEN

—◦—

Jesus answered, "It was neither that this man sinned,

nor his parents; but it was in order that the works of God

might be displayed in him. We must work the works of Him

who sent Me, as long as it is day;

night is coming, when no man can work.

While I am in the world,

I am the light of the world."

John 9:3-5 (NASB)

Some people are carefully hand-picked by God to display His works, His character, and His glory. They play an integral part in the Kingdom because their story declares His goodness. The greatness of these people is that their moral fiber is hewn from the rod of brokenness and the agony of sorrow. They did not choose the life that was dealt them, but rather God trusted them with displaying who He is in the midst of hard times.

These people are often obscure, unknown people - the ones bullied by the elite; the ones quieted by the religious; the ones whose names will never be remembered – but their story will live far beyond their life.

Such is the man blind from birth whose story is told in John chapter nine. He has no name. He is only known as the person associated with his problem – the blind man. In those days there was no public assistance program that would have provided a comfortable life for this man. Even his family, established in the synagogue, felt no obligation to cater to his disability. If this man was going to eat, he had to work for it. Uneducated with few opportunities open, he became the local beggar. His story says a lot about his character as beggar. He was diligent in his work and developed a reputation, as the neighbors and community knew him. He was faithful to his job although day after day he had to endure the condescending remarks from those passing by. Even on the day of Yeshua's arrival he could hear the disciples ask their teacher (as if he were not there) why he was as he was. All his life, he heard and probably believed that he was the product of sin.

As Yeshua passed by him that day – His disciples pointed him out and asked their teacher who was guilty for this man's dilemma. Yeshua's answer brings hope to every person who feels they are in a hopeless situation. Paraphrased, He responds to their lie-based thinking with, "This man is not a product of sin, but his story has great *worth* in the revealing of who God is!"[47]

This man had a divine experience with TRUTH. I've heard some teach that Yeshua combined his spittle and dirt because man originally comes from the ground and in this encounter; Yeshua grabbed the missing part, combined it with His own DNA, and applied it to the man's eyes. It sounds logical, but only God knows *how* spiritual things are manifested in the physical realm. All I know is that Yeshua applied dirt and spit to the problem area and that the man did not argue or complain when he was sent with mud caked on his eyes to the pool of Siloam to wash. He did what was asked and came back seeing!

---

[47] John 9:3

One would think that the community would throw a party and celebrate the wonderful works of our merciful God, right? Instead, this man faced an even greater test – that of accusation, interrogation, and excommunication. Even his own parents threw him before the court – fearing banishment from their church and friends. They chose their own comfort over their own son.

In an effort to discredit the divine miracle and the One who gave sight to this man, the Pharisaical court legally declared Yeshua to be a deviant and sinner opposed to God. I love the seeing-man's response! Although uneducated, he was street-smart (I am sure that as a beggar, he was privy to untold conversations as people passed by). He knew you would never win an argument with a legalist. So, he discounted their accusations and declared the simplicity of truth, "…one thing I do know, that, whereas I was blind, now I see."[48]

This infuriated the Pharisees, and they intensified the interrogation assailing him with contempt and insults with the intent to push this man to blaspheme. This style of attack, often used by bullies is called "ad-hominem" – which means you attack the other person when your argument is weak.

So, the man, in his street-smart sense, calmly turns the responsibility back upon the attackers and responds with, "You say that as disciples of Moses, you know all things spiritual; why is it you do not know where this miracle came from? Never before has it been recorded that anyone has opened the eyes of a person born blind. If this man were not from God, He could do nothing."[49] With that, the Pharisees hurled one more insult to the man – reminding him of his lowly position with them … then put him out.

What does he do now? A seeing man with no disability would suck as a beggar. Where will he go? The temple was the center of community for his people. Now he has no people. I can see him sitting somewhere on

---

[48] John 9:25
[49] John 9:30-33

the outskirt of the city feeling gutted with the words of the church leaders still ringing in his ears, *"You were born entirely in sin and are you teaching us? Who do you think you are?"*[50]

Yeshua heard what the religious people did to him and left to find this man with no people. What I love about God is that He is always willing to come to us in whatever "gutter" or low place we are in. He's not afraid to get His hands dirty with us.

He asks the man, "Do you believe in the Son of Man?"

The man responded, "Who is He, Sir, that I may believe in Him?" Yeshua said, [paraphrased] "You're looking at Him!" And a relationship was established. The man, who could see, now had community! This story of an un-named man has such simplicity of truth:

▶ You'll never win an argument with a legalist.

▶ When a legalist does argue with you, their attack is strongest when their argument is the weakest.

▶ When confronted with those who wish to revile and bully you, all you have to do is respond with what you know – nothing more.

▶ Faith was not criteria for this man's healing – only God's glory was. For those of us who struggle with doubt, this story ought to restore hope! This man didn't even know who the Son of Man was when he was healed!

▶ Jesus always finds a way to out-love us, even when we did nothing to deserve it.

▶ It doesn't matter what low place we find ourselves in – He will find us.

I've been in low places before; and if you are fortunate enough to be one of those chosen to display His wondrous works, you've been there, too

---

[50] John 9:34 (NASB)

(or will be one day). Some of these low places have been self-imposed – the result of wrong choices in search for love, acceptance, approval, and worth.

However, sometimes we are a casualty of circumstance. We are strategically placed in divine situations. These are often difficult places with difficult people. We are there to bring God into the story.

Such was the very, very cold winter night in Talkeetna, Alaska. My husband and I were asked to house-sit and tend to a dog-sled team while the owner of Fireweed Station took a trip to Russia. Since our cabin had no running water or electricity, we were thrilled to spend a few weeks at this lodge that had a shower, toilet, and lights.

This particular night was nearly a year after the drunk driver plowed into my husband at over 70 m.p.h. As mentioned earlier, Jesse's injuries included five ruptured disks in his back, three ribs separated from his spine, a broken collarbone and shoulder, a devastating frontal lobe [brain] injury, and his vision was reduced to 2% monocular [later he battled with blindness and wondered whether he would lose his vision permanently].

The most difficult of these to live with was the head injury. My husband could no longer channel pain because it lived in his head.

On several occasions, I found him curled up in a little ball with his hands desperately grasping his head. There were many days that he would vent all the pain and frustration at whoever was around him – usually me. One day he spewed out his pain at me for a nine-hour stretch. Although my mind understood, my soul was becoming embattled and weary.

On this particular dark and very cold night, we arrived at Fireweed Station after a long day's work, and we were tired. I don't know what set Jesse's short fuse off, but something did. He started in on me, blaming me for all his problems. His barbed words cut sharply. In his pain, he attacked my personhood, my identity, and my worth. There was no defense available, no mediator in the wilderness, and no pauses in his attack to reload. Destructive wave after wave poured over me. Inside I could feel myself breaking; almost short-circuiting. I reached a point where I was … done. There was nothing more in me – that was it … I was done.

I took off running out the cabin door into the blackness of winter night. We were miles away from anyone – no comforting arms, no refuge, and no escape. Not knowing anything else to do, I threw myself into a snowbank and begged God to die.

"I am at my end, O'God ... I am done! Take me because I can't take anymore! Oh my God, I am begging You – PLEASE take me home!"

My pleas were interrupted by Jesse still standing at the cabin door screaming at me – the pain in his head hurling more insults.

Tears were freezing to my face nearly as soon as they fell from my eyes. I begged fervently for divine intervention – wanting it all to end. I was in a very, very low place.

Then the Spirit of God showed up. I felt a strange stirring deep within my soul. A Word swirled about in my spirit, *"Fight"*. I had been emotionally numb for so long – enduring the assaults of all the men in my life, that I had no fight left in me. Nearly all my life, I only endured. I survived this long by enduring.

The Spirit's stirring brought to mind the little girl in me and I remembered a day that I had spunk. I didn't know how to fight anymore though. How do I fight against someone who lacks the capability to reason – whose brain only knows how to spew the pain?

"Fight", the Spirit said again.

Fine then, I'll fight (besides, I was getting very cold sprawled out in a snowbank with no jacket). So, I stood up, brushed myself off, and marched boldly over to my husband who was standing at the cabin door with anger etched all over his face. I stood before him on the steps, looked him in the eye, and said two of the foulest words I could think of.

For those of you who live with a brain-injured person, I understand your pain – but most importantly – never, ever do what I did. It elevated the intensity and Jesse let loose a litany of hurtful words that really cut to the core! With that, he slammed the door shut and left me standing shell-shocked in the cold.

I ran wildly back to the snowbank and threw myself in … again. I begged God over and over to take me. I even placed blame on Him, "See? I did what you told me to do – and look what happened!"

As cold set in, reminding me of my alive-ness - I pleaded more intensely.

That's when I heard from deep within the Spirit's question, *"Are you ready to fight My way?"*

Well, I was pretty dang cold by that time and if He wasn't going to take me, I was willing to try anything. Not knowing what I would do or what would happen, I pulled myself out of the snowbank and approached the cabin. It was then that a peace that passes all understanding enveloped me.

I calmly entered the living-room area and approached my husband – ignoring his icy glare. I looked him straight in the eye and said, **"I can never out-argue you, nor can I match your fury – but I can out-love you any day of the week!"**

With that, I turned and went to bed.

My husband will tell you that something changed in his head that night. After that he was more "aware". Whenever the pain and frustration became overwhelming and he would start to vent, he would look at me with an almost panic look in his eye and loudly proclaim, "I'M SORRY!" Then, a moment later, go right on vomiting pain.

However, as time progressed, these episodes became fewer and farther between. It took three long years for God to return my husband to me - a new and better man. Ever since that night in the cabin when I learned how to fight God's way, Jesse and I determined ourselves to out-love one another. Nearly twenty years later, we still say, "I love you" at the end of every phone conversation, every time we leave for work, and all spontaneous opportunities that pop up. We have come up with anomalies like:

"I love you."

"I love you, too, Honey."

"Well, I love you more."

"I love you the most."

"No, I love you more than most." Then we laugh.

Out-loving one another is also exhibited in the everyday things we do. Although we both know that it is not our responsibility to make one another happy (happiness is a choice), we strategically plan our day so that we minister to one another. Even though I work two jobs (teaching on the collegiate level) and come home late several nights a week, unplanned I will sit next to him on the couch with towel and oil and give my husband a foot massage. Sometimes during the day, I will unexpectedly text him a message like, "Wifey love Mongo" (my pet name for him because he is so strong).

My husband usually reserves his out-loving me to the bigger expressions in life. Recently, he fixed up our remote little cabin in the wilderness of Alexander Creek, Alaska. As a teacher, I often have to bring work home. As a writer, I crave the quiet places to pour words upon paper. In this itty-bitty cabin, he constructed a table, installed a sink and small stove, and wired in an outlet and generator to charge my computer – all so I could enjoy the adventure with him and operate in my calling.

In choosing to out-love, we are revealing who God is – His works, His character, and His goodness. In life, "it" is the determination to out- love that makes all the difference in the world!

Washing with the Water of the Word
CHAPTER FIFTEEN

"Husbands, love your wives,

just as Christ

also loved the church and gave Himself up for her;

that He might sanctify her,

having cleansed her by the washing of water

with the word..."

Ephesians 5:25-26 (NASB)

My husband, former rancher and world champion rodeo cowboy, is one of the best Shepherds I have ever known. He will tell you that, like King David, he learned most of his people skills by working with horses and cattle. He has a way of "reading" animals and people – dealing with the heart of matters instead of applying salve to symptoms. Some people find this personal intrusion offensive because he pries off the rusty padlocks of issues hidden in the dark chambers of their heart. At the same time, though, they appreciate that he did not patronize, flatter, or sweet-talk them. Most people appreciate the truth.

However, sometimes truth comes out of my husband in a real cowboy-kind of way. He doesn't fit the stereotype of most senior pastors. Instead of three-piece suits, he's my wrangler jean and cowboy boot man (Yep…mighty fine!). Our church has more men than women because Jesse is a man's man. In mentoring young men, he encourages them by example to stand strong, speak truth, and live the adventure.

Years ago, we were concerned about the climbing divorce rate of Christian families. In counseling others, Jesse and I discovered that many of these crumbling family units were the result of burn-out. They worked all week, on Saturdays they caught up on errands, shopping, and laundry – leaving Sunday as the only day to spend quality time together. However, if they attended Sunday church services, these families had very little time left to invest into each other. Therefore, we decided to have Friday night "Shabbat" services so that the families can spend the weekend doing things together as a unit.

Our church family does many things together in the Alaskan outdoors – camping, fishing, snowmobiling, hiking, canoeing – and our families are thriving. Men are learning how to be men, couples are learning how to have fun and work together, and the kids are learning what "healthy" relationship looks like.

It didn't always look like this. When we first started out in ministry, I wish we knew what we know now. Although we had wonderful teachers, some things you just have to learn by the school of hard knocks.

One of the hardest lessons had to do with our own relationship. Pastor's wives are some of the loneliest women in the world. We are usually known, not by our names, but as "the Pastor's wife" – and we have to share our husband with a whole community of needy people.

Distinguishing attributes about my husband that sets him apart from those that do not have a shepherd's heart is that he is accessible to the people and if someone is in a pit, he is willing to jump in that pit and stay as long as it takes to get them out. I, as a teacher, am more apt to stand at the top of the pit and remind them, "I taught you how to get out of there, now pull your big girl panties up and start acting like a lady (wife, mother, man, husband, father – whatever the case may be)."

Not my husband. No matter the hour, he will drag himself out of bed, drive through a blizzard, crash into a crack house and rescue young people (real story – we had death threats after that one), or simply just sit with someone in the hospital.

This can put a strain on a young relationship. In our early days, I would watch as he would tenderly anoint a person's forehead and pray passionately over them. While I was on visitation rounds with him, he would gently rub a patient's arms and legs to increase circulation or talk with them while giving them a foot rub. All this did my heart good.

One day, however, it was I who was sick. Before he left for work that morning, I asked him to pray for me. I was expecting the same kind and tender treatment he reserved for the flock. Instead, he awkwardly slapped my forehead and loudly pronounced, "Be healed!" With that, he turned and left.

I was too hurt to even cry. That single act spoke volumes about my worth as compared to the community he shepherded.

Throughout the next months the lie I believed as truth that day was validated over and over again. Instead of rubbing my back when it hurt or passionately caressing me, he would poke or jab and get angry when I didn't respond to his juvenile love language. (What I did not know until much, much later was that he was slow to mature in relationships because he did not receive the fatherly touch and affirmation growing up. No blame cast, though, because his father didn't receive it either.)

The more I harbored hurt feelings, the more I was aware of mounting offenses. One day a pastoral meeting was called at our large church and as an ordained minister, I showed up along with my husband. As the other pastors filtered in, the senior pastor looked my way and asked me to go get everyone coffee. A servant at heart, I complied with the request. When I returned with the urn and cups, Pastor met me at the door, took the tray, and asked me to sit in the waiting area. I was shocked and speechless when he shut the door in front of me. Fighting tears, I sat in the waiting room while all the other ministers (who happened to be men) took part in the pastoral meeting.

On the way home, Jesse couldn't understand why I was quiet and hurt over such a thing. He didn't see where there was a problem; therefore, I must be the problem. He accused me of making a mountain out of a mole hill, causing drama, and sowing dissention. By the time we got home, he was full-blown angry at me. A chill permeated the bedroom that night as silent tears poured from a broken heart.

The next morning as I made the 35-mile commute to work, I poured my heart out to God. Weeping, I lamented, "How can my husband blame *that* on me? How hard is it for him to just listen to me when I say my feelings hurt? What did I do to make him so angry? Father, what bothers me the most, though, is that my husband's opinion of me MATTERS!"

Immediately and (one of the few times in my life) audibly, Father's voice bellowed, *"HIS OPINION OF YOU MATTERS MOST TO ME!"*

That's the day I left all my stored up hurt at my Father's feet. How my husband thinks about me is most important to my Daddy, for He knows that out of the abundance of the heart, our mouth will speak.[51]

Words carry enormous power – they can cultivate and nurture or extinguish and destroy; they can heal or wound; they can lift up or tear down. Words don't go away when they leave our mouth, they are spiritually encapsulated and float through the air landing where they will. In the spirit in which they are sent is the seed that will be planted.

Paul understood the spiritual ramifications of the spoken word, especially in marriage relationships when he wrote to the church in Ephesus:

---

[51] Luke 6:45 "The good man out of the good treasure of his heart brings forth what is good; and the evil man out of the evil treasure brings forth what is evil; for his mouth speaks from the abundance in his heart."

For the husband is the head of the wife, as Christ also is the head of the church, He Himself being the Savior of the body. But as the church is subject to Christ, so also the wives ought to be to their husbands in everything. Husbands, love your wives, just as Christ also loved the church and gave Himself up for her; that He might sanctify her, having cleansed her by the washing of water with the word, that He might present to Himself the church in all her glory, having no spot or wrinkle or any such thing; but that she should be holy and blameless.

Ephesians 5:23-27(NASB)

For us to understand the triune spiritual mystery Paul is referring to, let's look at this passage in context. First, Paul says that "*...the husband is the head of the wife, as Christ also is the head of the church...*" The Greek word for "head" is "*kephale*" and it means "chief, source of life, headwater".

Contrary to those who would use this verse to dominate another person, the husband (representing Christ to his wife and the world) is the headwater (where things of life flow from) to his wife – just as Christ is the source of life to the church (His bride). Notice also in this verse that as the husband represents Christ, and the wife represents the church.

Just as the church responds to Christ's love, women respond to the life (or death) flowing from their husbands. If a woman is not responding favorably, what kind of water is flowing into her? Furthermore, how a man treats his wife (the mother of his children) will determine how she and the world watching feel about Yeshua and His character. People will either view Christ as full of love and grace or a harsh judge that controls and condemns – it all depends on how men in their lives treat women.

Paul then reiterates how the wife represents the church to her husband and to the world, "*But as the church is subject to Christ, so also the wives ought to be to their husbands in everything.*" He says just as the church is subject (the love language word: hupotassō – which means *willing* and *adaptable*) to Christ, so also the wives ought to be to their husbands in everything. Our actions toward and in response to our husband shows the world (and the church) how they ought to respond to Jesus! Do we look for ways to spend time with our husband? Are we willing to give the best we have to him? Do we maintain a positive attitude (*willing & adaptable*) in everything? The world ought to ask, "What is it about this man that she responds to him like that?"

In the next sentence, Paul addresses the men, "*Husbands, love your wives, just as Christ also loved the church and gave Himself up for her...*" The word for "love" is "*agapeō*" which means "direction of the will". He is saying, "Husbands, you may not feel like it all the time, you may not even like her very much right now but choose to love her with God's love." God's love is "*agape*" – the love that is needed. She needs your love and attention. She needs you to woo her, just as Jesus still courts the church.

▶ Jesus tends to our needs – without our even asking! Do we do this for each other?

▶ He tells us He has great plans for us and helps us cultivate our dreams! Husbands, do you cultivate your wife's dreams or are you a "sunshine killer" in her life – giving the impression that her only hope in this world is to watch you do what YOU want to do?

▶ He feels everything we do and cares enough to bottle our tears. Husbands do you listen to your wife or does it sound like a distant clanging symbol when she shares her heart with you?

▶ He accepts us just as we are and encourages us to grow. Remember, your wife's quirkiness is what makes her unique.

▶ He insists that we are significant and our lives have meaning and purpose.

▶ We matter, truly matter to Him.

▶ We are His garden. He nurtures and cultivates us.

▶ He sings over us as we sleep. Husbands, do you serenade your wife – or dance through the living room with her? My husband is a wonderful dancer. Whenever we are out dancing, I usually get a few rounds with him until all the old ladies in the room want to steal him for dances. In fact, we are together today because many years ago a cute little gal cut in on our dance and I got jealous!

Husbands, when you love your wives like Christ loves them, the result is "...[you] *sanctify her, having cleansed her by the washing of water with the word... "*[52] Let's address the second half of this sentence first, because it is by the husband's words that she is sanctified (set apart from the others). The man washes his wife with the watering of words. 'Word' here is *"rhema"* which means "to speak; a word spoken or uttered; stands for subject matter of the word, the thing which is spoken about".

A wife is her husband's garden. Just as Adam was taught how to nurture and cultivate a garden before Eve was introduced to him, a husband's job is to nurture and cultivate his wife. A wise gardener knows you have to feed the soil to gain the harvest. If a man sucks the life out of his wife, she will eventually die emotionally, find another source of worth, or just leave the jerk. However, if a man nourishes and cherishes her, she blooms like a rose. Everywhere she goes, she glows and emanates a sweet fragrance because of the way she has been treated by the men in her life. She truly believes she is somebody special. She stands out from the rest (sanctified). A husband's words have *that* much power! No wonder his opinion of his wife matters most to God!

Continuing with the passage in Ephesians five, Christ *longs* to, "... *present to Himself the church in all her glory, having no spot or wrinkle or any such thing... "* The Greek word for "present" is *"paristémi"* which means in this case "to place beside". He is looking forward to the day when the Bride sits next to Him in all her glory! The Greek word for "glory" is *"endoxos"*

---

[52] Ephesians 5:26

which means "splendid, regal, impressive, beautiful". So should a husband present (have beside him) a wife whose glory speaks well of him!

I often advise young women to spend time with a potential mate's family before she commits to a relationship. The way a man treats his mother will often be the way he treats his wife. Furthermore, as pastors, my husband and I usually try to observe how a couple interacts away from the church setting before we enter into counseling with them. Does the wife have a voice or does he answer for her? Does she hold her head high or is it hung in shame? Shame is the belief that something is wrong with them. An uncultivated wife will ultimately believe she is defective – that something is wrong with HER that causes her husband to treat her badly.

How a woman acts around her husband says volumes about *him*. She is his garden. (As a side note, please understand that we only observe in generalities. There are always exceptions to the general rule. Over the years we have seen cases of loving men who are tormented by women with bad issues. However, if we were to go back into the lives of these female tormentors, it is very probable that one could find specific instances where men have either failed them or there are mothers who taught their daughters to hate men. Sad. Nevertheless, the general rule is since women are responders, the wife is generally a good reflection of her husband.)

I like the woman I am today. Jesse and I have been through some pretty tough times together, but I would not go back and change anything. The only lingering regrets are when it took us so long to find God in our difficulty.

My husband, the wonderful Shepherd that he is, has finally worked past insecurity and trusts me enough to become vulnerable. When I need prayer now, he doesn't slap me on the forehead. (Thank, God!) And when I've had a rough day, he doesn't get angry and want to fix everything for me, he just gives me the hug that I desperately need. Most importantly, he sees me as his garden – a reflection of who he is – and he chooses which words to water me with. His opinion of me is a living likeness of him and "it" matters greatly to my Daddy what he thinks of me.

And the Two Become One
CHAPTER SIXTEEN

———————⌒———————

"So husbands ought also to love their own wives as their own bodies. He who loves his own wife loves himself; for no one ever hated his own flesh, but nourishes and cherishes it, just as Christ also does the church, because we are members of His body. For this cause a man shall leave his father and mother and shall cleave to his wife; and the two shall become one flesh."

Ephesians 5:28-31(NASB)

When the Bride sits next to Christ, she has no spot or wrinkle. I don't know about you, but I plan on having a long talk with God about age spots and wrinkles. However, on a positive note, I have *earned* every one of them! I just find it hard to look at a grandma standing in the mirror when I feel thirty inside!

Spots and wrinkles, although seen on the outside, start on the inside. The Greek word for "spot" is "*spiloo*" and it means, "defiled". Jesus is very concerned about our inner health and well-being. It is His desire to have a Bride next to Him that is beautiful, radiate, and not worn down and tattered emotionally. He wants His Bride to know who she is and the value she has!

He also desires His Bride to be, *"holy and blameless"*. The Greek word for "holy" is *"haglos"* which means, "set apart, pure". I Peter 1:15-16 says, *"... but like the Holy One who called you, be holy yourselves also in all your behavior because it is written, 'You shall be holy for I am holy."*

Many of us misunderstand what "holy" means. Over the years we have been chastised by the ultra-religious for laughing in the sanctuary, skiing on Sunday, playing a secular song in worship service, wearing jeans to church, and even for saying "crap" one time. Yeshua wants His bride to be holy, but if the aforementioned were the criteria for "holy" – His wife sounds … boring.

Looking at the true meaning of the word *"haglos"*, it simply means his wife is pure in heart. She is free to be herself. She has no ulterior motive in her actions. Jesus himself said, *"Blessed are the pure in heart, for they shall see God."*[53] The Bride, free to be her unique quirky self, shall sit next to God!

My husband married a "quirk". Sometimes I think that I am not quite what he imagined in a wife. Some aspects of my unique personality he has struggled to understand are:

- I love rocks. We have rock walls in our home, rocks on shelves, and even rock 'gardens'. Each one tells a story and one day I am going to sit down with the Creator and have Him tell me the tale of each one.

- I am a treasure hunter. Each day is an adventure as I hunt out the treasure He has hidden for me.

- I am a truth-bearer. I love TRUTH and abhor secrets. I believe in dealing with "white elephants" in the room so that we can deal honestly with one another.

- I'm not concerned where the appropriate worship place is – I just worship. I have spontaneously sang in service, lifted my

---

[53] Matthew 5:8

eyes on rivers while fishing, held my hands up to the heavens on mountaintops, and danced before my Father in the privacy of my home.

• I pick up pennies. If He can't trust me with a little, how in the world is He going to trust me with a lot?

• I pick up litter. Although a little humbling at times, we are stewards of the earth.

• I can't sleep if there is a wrinkle in the sheet.

• In order ... I dress by putting on sock shoe, sock shoe – not the other way of sock, sock, shoe, shoe.

• I freely talk about any issue with my spiritual kids. I want them to be healthy in all areas.

• I like red wine, apples with peanut-butter, and chew gum almost all the time.

• I have texture issues with food. Anything that resembles a booger is off limits.

• I am organized and love organization. This is very hard when this kind of person marries a visionary. The visionary has their eye on goals not on the dirty socks around the room.

• I am frugal. I cut dryer sheets in thirds, wash and re-use Ziploc bags, and eat leftovers.

I am sure my husband got more than he bargained for when he won my heart. But he will tell you today that it is all the idiosyncrasies that make me interesting to him – I am his beautiful MESS! Together, though, we complement each other, and, in the Kingdom, we sure do make one great team! It's no wonder Jesus told the disciples that they need to know who they are if they want to be effective in spiritual matters. In Matthew 17, when the disciples could not cast out a demon, they brought the matter before Jesus. He explained to the disciples, it was *"because of the littleness of your faith; for truly I say to you, if you have faith **as a mustard seed**, you shall say to this mountain, 'Move from here to there,' and it shall move; and nothing shall be impossible to you[54]."*

We must believe *as* a mustard seed believes. What does a mustard seed know? It only knows one thing … that it's a tiny little mustard seed. When you plant the mustard seed, it will grow into a mustard plant – not a banana tree – but a mustard plant.

Yeshua was telling them if you know who you are, you will be able to accomplish anything. When you put two people together who know who they are – including their greatness, their quirks, and their imperfections – nothing shall be impossible!

Although Paul wasn't married, he knew how important it was for the husband to look at his wife, see her for who she is, and speak that greatness into her. He said, *"So husbands ought also to love their own wives as their own bodies. He who loves his own wife loves himself; for no one ever hated his own flesh, but nourishes and cherishes it, just as Christ also does the church, because we are members of His body. For this cause a man shall leave his father and mother and shall cleave to his wife; and the two shall become one flesh."[55]* To be an effective team, each spouse needs a healthy partner.

Just as wives *ought* to be willing and adaptable to their husbands in everything,[56] the husbands *ought* to love their wives. Paul's use of the word "ought" tells me that as a general rule, husbands are not loving their wives as themselves and the wives are not responding well. It makes no sense to Paul that they are not.

Therefore, Paul quotes Moses and says a man should leave his father, mother, and everything that is familiar to him so that he can cleave (glue himself to) his wife. As a man nourishes (provides her with all the things

---

[54] Matthew 17:19-21
[55] Ephesians 5:28-31
[56] Ephesians 5:24

needed to live and causes her to develop and grow stronger) and cultivates (tenderly tends to her), he wins! Not only will he have a beautiful, spotless Bride on his arm, but she (as a responder) will respect and admire him! To Paul, it only makes sense to do so.

Paul then addresses the wives, "…and let the wife *see to it* that she respects her husband."[57] Wives *ought* to be making every effort to respond respectfully to her husband as he becomes vulnerable, leaving everything familiar, to cultivate her. This implies that this act is a CHOICE. It's responding to our husbands with a thank you, a back rub, an atta-boy! Unfortunately, many women are still allowing old wounds to fester, and men have no safe place to be vulnerable. Just as love is a choice for men, respect is a choice for women. Sometimes we simply need to deal with old injuries (issues), pull up our big girl panties, and get on with life. "It's" not all about you – it is about the success of US.

Sanctity of the Moment
CHAPTER SEVENTEEN

———————⌇———————

"Restore to me the joy of Your salvation,

And sustain me with a willing spirit"

Psalm 51:12

The marriage kiss marks the moment when the two are in "it" for the long-haul – through thick and thin, better or worse. God does not promise that it is going to be easy or that life will be fair. But rather, in this triune relationship I think God desires that we experience excruciatingly hard times so that we develop history together. I like to think of it as "His-story" because God is with us – feeling everything we do – we just need to look for Him in all things.

History is the fortress of a strong relationship. I am not threatened by young pretty women who flirt with my husband (not happy with it, but definitely not threatened) because Jesse and I have history – stories of devastation, starting all over again, living with no electricity or running water, sickness, despair, … and jubilation! We have proof of each other's character, steadfastness, and loyalty. We have obtained the evidence of trust despite what is going on around us. Somehow, someway we know we will make it through the storm.

With each storm comes a beautiful revelation of God. The Book of Exodus (actually called the Book of Shamōt – the Book of Names), is not a book of the Israelites' journey round and round the mountain for forty years and all their trials, but a book about God revealing His character, His love, and who He is to the people. He is still in the business of using difficult times to reveal Himself to us.

In the spring of 2015, like King David once did, I poured out my heart to Abba Father to restore unto me the joy of His salvation.[58] I was in a funk. In my marriage, church, and work – I was simply going through the motions – emotionally detached. I wanted to *feel* again, to embrace life, and to be enthusiastic about something. I felt like I was living in a perpetual pity party, my dreams on hold while I served those around me and tended to all my responsibilities (that's what grown-ups do). I knew that I couldn't stay in that mode much longer because we can only minister out of our overflow – not our need.

In my forty-mile commute that morning, I wept. *"Lord, restore unto me the joy of your salvation - the joy of relationship with Jesus!"* In my mind, I was asking for revelation or a spoken word or even a supernatural "zap" that would pull me out of my funk. Instead, in His agapé-type of love (the giving of what is needed), He set into motion a series of events.

That July, Jesse and I went out four-wheeling with another couple in Eureka, Alaska about 125 miles into the wilderness. It is one of my favorite places in the world. For years, I told my husband, "If something happens to me, stand on top of Monument Hill and just let my ashes go with the wind." It is a place where one can see ... eternity.[59]

The Nelchina River flows through this panoramic valley. This July it happened to be a mighty rushing river loaded with glacial melt and there was no ideal place to cross it with the four-wheelers, so we stopped on a trail about a 30-foot incline up from the river. After a bite of picnic lunch,

---

[58]   Psalm 51:12

[59]   See back cover for photo taken at the beginning of this trip – Jesse, Jena, and I standing on top of Monument Hill.

our friends and Jesse worked on preparing the rods for grayling fishing. As usual, I poked around for rocks as our beloved English-Setter dog, Jena, excitedly explored new territory.

Making my way down the steep decline to the river, I poked through the brush looking for fossil rocks – then, out of the corner of my eye, I spotted something white bobbing along the bank in the river. Our dog had fallen into the raging water! The strong current had pushed her into over-hanging branches, and she was drowning. In a matter of nanoseconds, I plotted my strategy to rescue her. Then, without hesitation, I jumped in, and as planned, shoved her toward the shore. Within seconds, though, my hip waders and rain gear filled up with water and sucked me under (I know, I know...Alaskans know better than to jump into a raging river with all their gear on!) I grabbed an overhanging branch and yelled for help because nobody knew I was IN the river. However, the branch broke, and the strong current sucked me down river. Fighting with all my might, I was able to grab hold of another overhanging branch and yell for help again. This time, Jesse and our friends, Neil and Lindy, heard "something". Unfortunately, the current ripped me from my stronghold and carried me downstream again. During all this, the rational thought that occurred to me was, *"This is serious - really serious. You may not make it out of here. You have to yell louder."* Not to mention the random, but clear thoughts, *"Your husband needs you. You have no one to teach your classes, you must make it back."* For most my life I have been a "scrapper", able to work my way out of situations. However, this time I wasn't sure if I was going to make it out.

Swept under the mighty current, I reached frantically overhead for anything to grab. Finally, I managed to catch hold of another overhanging branch and screamed with all my might. This time they heard my cry for help; however, their immediate thought was that a bear had gotten hold of me - and they came running toward the scream with guns drawn.

The river sucked me under once again, but I held tight onto the branch. Not long after that, I felt a strong hand grab hold of me. My husband, my beloved hero, pulled me up out of the mighty raging river! Once on the bank, they immediately shucked my cold wet clothing and offered up dry warm clothes and boots to prevent hypothermia.

A precious moment came after the treacherous re-climb of Monument Hill (on our 4-wheelers). At the top, I knelt before my Creator and thanked Him for many things, including the opportunity for more days to live, to love, and to work. Although it took seven hours before we finally made it home, our dog (Jena) and I were fine - a little traumatized - but fine. God is good!

My husband, Jesse, later told the church that although he would have grieved losing Jena, he would have greatly missed the "words" if he had lost me in that river. What a wonderful thing...to not only appreciate the unique traits and quirks of each other, but to treasure conversation and the time spent with one another - in relationship.

A week after that incident, I was driving home in the Alaska mid- night sun from Friday night service with my dear sweet spiritual daughter, Yasmin. Making our way along the Glenn Highway toward Palmer, we approached the Echo Lake area. From out of nowhere, with no warning, two young men riding "crotch rockets" (high-speed motorcycles) sped past and cut in front of me, missing my car by less than two inches. It was later estimated that they were doing in excess of 140 mph. No sooner had I caught my breath from being startled, than we crowned the knoll and came upon a horrific fiery inferno. I can't even begin to describe the scene before us. The two motorcyclists had run into an SUV that had pulled out onto the road. As the first one there, I ran from victim to victim assessing their need. The driver of the SUV was walking around with his hands held to the sides of his head trying to make sense of what happened. His left eye was dangling on his cheekbone. A woman in the SUV was screaming for help as the man in the passenger's seat was bleeding profusely. A young man, badly broken was lying on the side of the road next to a blazing motorcycle.

As people arrived at the scene, I yelled to them, "There's another motorcyclist somewhere – FIND HIM!" I then knelt next to the one nearest me. I prayed and I spoke softly to him (trying to disregard how broken up he was). I told him that it was okay, he was not alone. He took a long breath in … then exhaled. By the Grace of God, that was his last breath.

By then, the State Troopers and local Police arrived, and they took over assessing the horrendous scene. Both young men lost their life that night… and I wept. Later that week, I wrote to the parents of the young man I sat with:

Sometimes in life I question where God is at. The loss and grief seem so great that I lose sight of the Giver of breath. In the sanctity of this very moment, I sit and gaze at a cloud-filled sky that hides the beauty of Pioneer Peak. I know in my heart that the mountain is still there – but I cannot see it. It is the same with God. Sometimes we can't see Him. But He is still there. My name is Bobette Stubblefield, and I was the first person to your son. I arrived within seconds. I want you to know that he was not alone. I sat with him and prayed over him. Within minutes others arrived, and we sat with your boy and honored the sanctity of his life.

As a mom who sent one of her sons to war, I can only imagine your sorrow – and I grieve with you. Your son's face is forever etched in my mind. I want you to know that there was a supernatural Peace present as the Giver repossessed the breath of your son. I pray that this same Peace that passes all understanding envelops you through this most difficult time.

Two weeks after this heart-wrenching event our beloved cat of seventeen years, Kramer, passed away. And I wept… again.

A week after that, I found myself in another intense situation. When class was over at the college where I teach and most the students exited the classroom, without provocation one of the male students threw something at another male student. Before I could diffuse the situation, the fight was on. Tables were toppled and chairs tossed to and fro. I ran into the hall and sent a lingering student for help – then ran back into the classroom. At one point, the one attacked held the attacker down and we really thought the fight was over with. However, when he let go, the attacker headed aggressively back. It was at that point that I reached out and grabbed hold of his shirt and tried to order him back. But he jerked violently, and my arm became hyper-extended. He then swung at the other young man, missing him – but hitting my arm.

Soon thereafter, enough help arrived to diffuse the situation. After some tense moments, everyone left the room but me, the attacker, and the Director of Education. After a brief assessment, the Director of Education told the attacker that he needed to leave the campus immediately. Boldly, the "mama" in me over-rode his decision and told the attacker that he first needed to straighten up my room before he left.

As I directed where each table and chair went, I spoke to him saying, "Son, I don't know what was going through your head today, but you hurt me." (I later found out that he tore my rotator cuff.) He responded, "I'm sorry, Miss Bobette."

Within a week of this incident, I opened my email and found urgent correspondence from my stepsister in Seattle, Washington – to call her as soon as possible. At first, I didn't recognize the name. For years I (lovingly?)[60] referred to my stepsisters as Drusilla and Anastasia – and I honestly had forgotten their real names. When I called Drusilla (of course, not her real name), she informed me that my biological dad had ordered all his affairs that day; then stepped out onto the front lawn of their home and shot himself in the head. Stunned, I wasn't sure how to process this information.

It's not like we were really close. I tried to have a relationship with my father – my husband even moved our family to Seattle in the year 2000 so

---

[60] I questioned later in life why I had thought of my stepsisters as Cinderella's doted-on sisters. There was really no logical answer other than I knew in my heart that I was the sister held at a distance, not fully accepted into the family. However, rather than holding onto animosity or hard feelings, I love and honor them for the years of tending to my estranged biological father.

that we could get to know him better. However, one day he and my step-mother drove by and saw a thirteen-year-old young man mowing our yard. Upset, my dad called a family meeting with my stepmother, stepsisters, and their husbands. It was unanimously decided that Jesse and I were ... acting irresponsibly.

On Monday morning when I arrived at work, my dad was waiting for me. He informed me that our current behavior was unacceptable and that we needed to take responsibility for our own yard. I responded with, "I am in my forties, I have raised two children, and if I want to hire a young man to mow our yard, that is MY prerogative." For the next half hour, he berated and tried to shame me into thinking I had let the family down. I finally informed him that he was causing me to steal from my employer (by handling personal affairs on company time) and that he would have to leave the premises, or I would have to call security. And he left.

Loving my father was easier from a distance. So, when the funeral was arranged soon after his death, I contacted my stepsisters and told them that I was going to honor their position as daughters in my father's life and I would not show up and upset the apple cart as the "token" daughter.

Two weeks went by before I received the official decree from the courts that stated in black and white that although my brother and I were the biological children of my dad, ALL assets were to go to my stepmother, Drusilla, and Anastasia. Neither my brother nor I expected anything from our father's estate ... but, to read *"REJECTED"* in an official document was another matter. *"Thanks, Dad. Was that really necessary?"* was all I could think. Although it stung, I was ultimately grateful that I had a healthy relationship with my heavenly Father.

I was also thankful at that time that Jesse was immersed in his job as manager of the equestrian and farm areas of the Alaska State Fair. Fair activities occupy a lot of his time, and this allowed me the alone time to spend with Abba Father and mend. It just so happened that he had brought in a medieval jousting show this late summer of 2015. There was an immediate connection between these medieval knights and my world-champion cowboy husband. Before long, they had him competing in the jousting games with them. Jesse was having a grand ole' time competing and working horses again.

Unbeknown to us, though, was this activity – combined with 140 pounds of armor – was aggravating old rodeo injuries to his hip area. After two weeks of competing, he developed a sepsis infection on the bruised bone in his left hip. By the end of the fair, it was obvious that he didn't feel well and was extremely tired. Soon thereafter, the infection reached the surface of his buttock area. Once at the surface, the septic infection turned into MRSA.

One day, as we were house-hunting, I noticed he was running a fever and that he was struggling to keep up with the day. I said, "Honey, forget a house today, we are going to the Urgent Care."

The doctor, a former field medic, did immediate in-office surgery on him – digging deep into the hip area. The lidocaine did little to ease Jesse's pain. He buried his face into the pillow and moaned. I, on the other hand, starting tasting "metal" and felt hot – very hot. Noticing this, the doctor stopped digging into my husband's wound and ordered me to lie down.

Really wanting to comfort my husband, I resisted. Moments later, though, I realized that I was going to be of no good unless I followed doctor's orders.

So now, flat on the floor, I looked up at Jesse's pained face and knew I could offer no comfort to him. The doctor kept working on the infected area. Come to find out, the MRSA was precariously close to his colon and femoral artery. Had we waited two days, I would have been planning his funeral.

The next day, we had to come back and have the wound cleaned out all over again. It was déjà vu – I started tasting "metal" and the room got extremely hot… this time, however, I looked at Doc and said, "I know the drill…" and obediently lay on the floor.

Doc put Jesse on a cocktail of drugs to kill any remnants of the MRSA infection. Unfortunately, these poisons crippled my husband's immune system. Months later, he is still not well. Not knowing what else to do, I hold on to Him whose name is Love. Our lives are in His hands.

A couple of weeks after the MRSA episode, I noticed that Jena (our beloved dog of eight years) was not feeling well. That morning as I got ready for work, instead of her happy self – she just laid there and watched me. When I kissed my husband goodbye for the day, I mentioned that Jena was not acting her normal self.

Only hours into my morning class at school, I received a message from Jesse saying, "PRAY - IMPORTANT – PRAY!" By the time he got Jena to the veterinarian, she had all but bled out from an internal tumor. We had no time to prepare for her dying. Weeks before, I had risked my life to save her – but now, there was nothing I could do. Within moments … she was gone.

It's hard to explain the depth of attachment to those who don't have pets. Our pets have always been an integral part of the family. Losing Jena was equivalent to losing a daughter. She went everywhere with us – she had her own employment badge at my husband's work, she went to church with us, and she accompanied him on ministry calls. Life without her felt empty - not only for us, but also for all those around us.

In October for Pastor Appreciation month, the members of our church and those at the fairgrounds who work with my husband took a collection and raised money to purchase us another English-Setter puppy. "Sam" (short for Samantha, which means "God hears") is the newest member of our family. I question God about her name because at 14 weeks, it is like having a toddler on "crack" in our home. She is loving, inquisitive, strong-willed, ornery, energetic, smart, and beautiful – all in one package.

As winter announced its approach, depositing "termination dust" on the surrounding mountains, I realized that Abba Daddy had answered my desperate request to restore unto me the joy of Salvation [Yeshua]. I value each and every moment now and realize that ***ultimate joy is the totality of living in the fullness of every moment with Him.*** If He is in the moment, there is Goodness in that moment. I call it the "Sanctity of the Moment".

Since then, my morning prayer is:

> *"Lord, fully embrace and envelope me into the sanctity of your moment – I want to know the fullness of YOU – particle by particle, spirit by spirit. I want to come in tune with Your heart- beat on all matters, see through Your eyes and hear through Your ears. I long to think with Your thoughts and act in Your ways. I want to smell You and smell like You. Allow me to be the dispenser of You throughout each and every moment of the day, dispensing Your love, kindness, wisdom ... and Your smell everywhere that I go.*

So here I sit, months later, in a cabin out in the wilderness of Alaska on another adventure with my husband. Just getting out here was like living life on the edge of eternity. I encountered a wolf today (who thankfully went on his way) and fought trepidation when a shelf of ice on the river dropped a few inches as we crossed it. But we made it, and I wouldn't trade "it" for anything.

It is night and I am listening to my husband softly snore. He and our newly beloved "Sam" are curled up together in a sleeping bag. I sit at the plywood table he made for me with a battery light, and I write. Life is good.

I can only hope that from here on out, we never have to "preach" of the relationship with the Bridegroom we love so much – but rather, we just live "it" – the love, adventure, laughter, hope, and joy. The mystery that Paul talks about in Ephesians 5:32 is the revelation of relationship between that of a man and a woman and how "it" displays the love relationship that Christ has for us. Our moment-to-moment living speaks volumes to the world around us. When we can be *real* with ourselves, *real* with each other, and *real* with God – life is Good.

In closing, for years I have studied, meditated, and searched for the depth of what it means to be fully engaged in the "sanctity of the moment". Other than being immersed in devastation and learning how to embrace Him in all situations, the BEST answer I have received came from my spiritual daughter, Kat Hubble. She wrote for me the following poem:

The Sanctity of the Moment

Rise to the task of the moment

Not the task, but the essence

In full attunement, pay attention

Not strained focus

Open eyes

And open heart

Take in gray, modeled mountains

Vast cerulean sky with dead fall trees

This arrangement of cloud and colors never to exist again

The moment is free

It contains no apology

It is complete

Sacred

Sanctuary for "I AM"

Not "I was" or "I will be if you get it right"

In Creator's palms

See a speck of sparkling magic

A snowflake. Crystal unique

Kiss to be blown

Gift to be cherished

In a second, melted.

No future exists without this gift

Fixed on the future, the gift perishes unreceived

Open your eyes

Do you see the moment?

One heartbeat unto life

DNA unto destiny

Complete in God's wonderful nature

And nature knowing completely the wonder within

"It" is the wedding kiss.